The
EVERYTHING®
Palmistry Book

Dear Reader:

When you first look at someone's hands, you are in essence looking into a soul with a magnifying glass. Deeper lines can tell you where a person has been and where they are going; finer lines can tell you more about all the challenges and obstacles he or she has encountered along the way. Does palm reading contain all the answers to the major questions in life? No—but it is a fabulous tool that allows you to begin looking for outward evidence of your inward journey.

My family has held on to its Turkish and Greek folklore, which includes the reading of hands, cards, tealeaves, and Turkish coffee grounds. My maternal grandmother was very adept at matching couples based on palm reading and looking at a strong cup of Turkish coffee; several happy couples can attribute their marital longevity to *Yia-Yia* (Greek for "Grandma") and her skill in reading the lines on their hands to determine the perfect match.

Today, I am proud of my family lineage and continue these practices as a metaphysician. Over the past fifteen years, I have read hundreds of palms, and I feel highly qualified (and honored) to share my unique experience and insights with you.

Katina Z. Jones

Welcome to the EVERYTHING® Series!

These handy, accessible books give you all you need to tackle a difficult project, gain a new hobby, comprehend a fascinating topic, prepare for an exam, or even brush up on something you learned back in school but have since forgotten.

You can choose to read an *Everything*® book from cover to cover or just pick out the information you want from our four useful boxes: e-questions, e-facts, e-alerts, and e-ssentials.

We give you everything you need to know on the subject, but throw in a lot of fun stuff along the way, too.

We now have more than 400 *Everything*® books in print, spanning such wide-ranging categories as weddings, pregnancy, cooking, music instruction, foreign language, crafts, pets, New Age, and so much more. When you're done reading them all, you can finally say you know *Everything*®!

QUESTIONS?
Answers to
common questions

FACTS
Important snippets
of information

ALERTS!
Urgent
warnings

ESSENTIALS
Quick
handy tips

PUBLISHER Karen Cooper

DIRECTOR OF ACQUISITIONS AND INNOVATION Paula Munier

MANAGING EDITOR, EVERYTHING SERIES Lisa Laing

COPY CHIEF Casey Ebert

ACQUISITIONS EDITOR Lisa Laing

DEVELOPMENT EDITOR Elizabeth Kassab

EDITORIAL ASSISTANT Hillary Thompson

Visit the entire Everything® series at *www.everything.com*

THE
EVERYTHING®
PALMISTRY
BOOK

Discover what the future holds—
life, love, and wealth—all in
the palm of your hand

Katina Z. Jones

Adams Media Corporation
Avon, Massachusetts

For John, Lilly Elenis, Madelyn Dela,
Zoe Quan Yin, and Sammi Jo

An Everything® Series Book.
Everything® and everything.com® are registered trademarks of F+W Publications, Inc.

Published by Adams Media, an F+W Publications Company
57 Littlefield Street, Avon, MA 02322 U.S.A.
www.adamsmedia.com
ISBN 10: 1-58062-876-1
ISBN 13: 978-1-58062-876-1
Printed in the United States of America.

J I H G F E

Library of Congress Cataloging-in-Publication Data
Jones, Katina Z.
The everything palmistry book / Katina Z. Jones.
p.   cm.   (An everything series book)
ISBN 1-58062-876-1
1. Palmistry. I. Title. II. Everything series.

BF921.J66 2003
133.6–dc21

2002154918

This book is available at quantity discounts for bulk purchases.
For information, call 1-800-289-0963.

Contents

Acknowledgments

Special thanks to Bethany Brown at Adams Media and Cindy Grahl of Word Wizards for their editorial guidance and assistance.

Top Ten Things You Can Learn
from Palmistry

1. How to look closely into the lines on your hand for deeper meaning.

2. The possibilities that lie ahead in your future.

3. Your basic personality traits, tendencies, and talents.

4. What you need in order to live a long, happy, and healthy life.

5. The timing of your life's major events.

6. Your place in the Universe and your spiritual destiny.

7. How to read the signs to avert potential obstacles or problems in your life.

8. What you need in order to achieve success in romance—and what to look for in a potential partner.

9. Your health "trouble spots" and how to best care for your body and spirit.

10. Hidden talents that could bring you happiness and success.

Introduction

▶IT'S OFTEN SAID THAT THE EYES ARE THE WINDOWS of the soul, but in many ways, it's the hands that offer the greatest insights into who we are and what we can become. As distinctive as the genetic code that sets us apart from every other individual on the planet, each human hand contains unique lines that tell a unique and personal story. No two of us are the same when it comes to palms and fingerprints.

This is where the art of palmistry comes in. An intuitive practice that dates back more than 1,000 years, palmistry is the study of the lines, texture, shapes, and idiosyncrasies of the hand. It is not limited to the palm area alone, but also includes the fingers, knuckles, wrists, mounts, joints, and overall shape of the hand itself. Palmistry can tell you the past, but it can also tell you about future possibilities. As it is practiced today, palmistry offers a complete personality profile of an individual, including his or her major life choices, challenges, and opportunities.

When a professional palm reader looks at your hand, he or she is looking for patterns as well as answers to the great questions of life. Will you live a long and happy life? Will you find love? What kind of career might you choose? How successful will you be? Will you enjoy good health throughout most of your life?

You can get answers to life's bigger questions in a half-hour reading done by an experienced palm reader, but you don't need a professional to tell you the future that lies in your own hands. With a little helpful guidance from this book, you can read palms for yourself, your family, and friends. For centuries, thousands of people have done just that—as serious means of prediction, a parlor game, or a method of gaining insight, perspective, or direction in life.

This book will help you see, perhaps for the first time, the blueprint of your own life and will also offer understanding and insight into the lives of others around you. You will see striking correspondence between the lines on your hand and the paths you've already chosen. You will discover what lies ahead in the creases and seemingly insignificant markings on the palms of both of your hands. To help you learn how to interpret each line and mount in every part of your hands, more than 100 illustrations and examples are provided.

You will also discover palmistry's rich history and will find out how it "joins hands" with other intuitive arts, such as psychic readings, tarot cards, chakra reading, and the ancient Chinese oracle known as the *I-Ching*, or Book of Changes.

Your hands contain helpful information about your talents, emotions, dreams, and spirituality, but you should always remember that they are like a road map full of many choices that can affect your destiny. Your life's lessons are already written in the lines on your hand, but there is not always a clear-cut, predestined path. The road ahead will certainly have some forks and crossroads, and it will be up to you to decide where you want to go. However, with the help of palmistry, you can embark on your life's journey with a map of your destiny—right in the palm of your hand!

Chapter 1

Palmistry: The Past and the Present

Palmistry is an ancient tradition with a long, rich history. Its origins may be traced back to India or China, but it was adapted by many cultures, which then shaped and expanded this practice to fit their own knowledge and beliefs. Through the centuries, palm reading evolved into the metaphysical art it is today. This chapter offers a brief overview of the history of palmistry, as well as some basic information on what palmistry is and what you should know if you are looking for a good palm reader.

Earliest Origins

The human hand has probably been a source of mystery and fascination since the beginning of human existence, as evidenced by the drawings of early cave dwellers and the personal thumbprint stamps of the ancient Chinese emperors. But even though there are hundreds of artifacts depicting interest in the hand itself, there are few written texts referring specifically to the metaphysical art of palmistry.

FACT

Palmistry is mentioned in ancient Sanskrit, Vedic, and Semitic texts. There are references to palm reading in the Bible, and detailed paintings of hands on cave walls. Although no written records exist, historians believe that palmistry was studied in Tibet, Persia, Egypt, and Babylonia. Legend has it that Aristotle found a golden scroll with hand-reading instructions on an altar to the messenger god Hermes.

Palmistry is one of the oldest forms of divination or seeing into the future, and can be traced back to China and India, with evidence of regular practice dating as far back as 3200 B.C. Through migration and expansion, the practice of palmistry spread to Persia, the Middle East, and then to Greece and the rest of Europe, although the Europeans did not openly accept it until the eighteenth century.

Palmistry in Europe

Many believe that palm reading in Europe became popular because of the gypsies, who are still associated with this practice. Gypsy fortune-telling methods enjoy a long and often colorful history, and many gypsies still read palms today, especially in Europe.

But this practice was not always accepted by the mainstream cultures of Europe. In fact, there have been many times when palm readers and other practitioners of the occult were persecuted for their practices, which ran counter to Christianity and were believed by some to be closely related to sorcery and witchcraft. In times of Christian zealotry, practices such as palm reading would be conducted in secret, but they were never forgotten.

Napoleon and the Hand of Fate

In the eighteenth century, palmistry experienced a revival in France, where it enjoyed tremendous popularity in elite circles. Napoleon himself was a believer, and consulted regularly with Madame Marie Anne Adelaide Lenormand, a card and palm reader who had come to Paris when she was twenty-one years old.

Napoleon often sought Madame Lenormand's advice in political and personal matters; he visited her in the salon she shared with a Madame Gilbert. In fact, Madame Lenormand's main claim to fame was her predictive ability regarding Napoleon and Josephine. Unfortunately, Napoleon didn't always heed her words of advice, a mistake that likely led to his ultimate demise.

Madame Lenormand kept a written record of her divination methods and results. Fortunately, these records have been preserved and continue to be published today.

ESSENTIAL

Palmist and author William Benham believed that our own will and the Divine Mind of God jointly form the lines on our hands, etching our personal pictures of destiny in a place where we could easily access them. However, it is important to realize that you always have free will and the choice to avoid negative situations.

Resurgence of Palmistry in Victorian England

The turn of the nineteenth century in England saw the revival of spiritualism and a growing interest in paranormal studies, which in turn led to the a renaissance for palmistry. Victorians were keenly interested in removing boundaries from the mind, and they actively sought unusual means of doing so.

Palmistry's revival was led by the charismatic performer Count Louis von Hamon, who was widely known as Cheiro the Palmist (the name derives from *kheir,* the Greek word for hand). Known all over Europe and America for his amazingly accurate readings and flamboyant style, Cheiro was the first professional palmist to assimilate all of the previous teachings into one methodology. He gleaned the best elements of Greek, Indian, and other Asian and European hand-reading techniques and created his own detailed guides so that palmistry could move from private parlors to the masses. Cheiro's groundbreaking *Guide to the Hand* (published in 1897) and several related books are still in print today (see Appendix B for additional bibliography).

Modern Uses

Today, the study of the lines and patterns on the hand has many applications in addition to the art of palmistry. Based on the work of seventeenth-century physicians like Nehemiah Grew and Jan Purkinjie, both of whom lectured and wrote extensively about the uniqueness of fingerprints, modern physicians have been able to develop interesting parallels between hand types and physical challenges or illnesses like Down's Syndrome or even cancer.

ESSENTIAL

The hand is a critical component of the human body. We have more than 200 million nerve fibers in our brains, and a significant number of these are exclusively connected with the hand.

Many psychologists recognize the correlation between specific lines and patterns on the fingers and hands and well-defined personality characteristics. Carl Jung, one of the founders of psychoanalysis, believed that palmistry is the outward appearance of secrets we try to keep under lock and key in our subconscious minds. Another noted psychologist, Charlotte Wolff, believed that "the hand is a visible part of the brain"; she even diagnosed many of her patients using hand-reading techniques.

Criminologists often rely on the work of palmists to develop criminal profiles along with other pieces of forensic evidence derived from crime scenes. While some rely on their own intuition in reading the marks on a criminal's hands, others call in specialists known as investigative psychics in order to develop fuller, more complete pictures of those involved in criminal investigations.

FACT

As you know, police work depends on the uniqueness of fingerprints and handprints to properly identify a victim or criminal. The process of fingerprinting as we know it today began in 1901 and was used by Scotland Yard for investigative purposes—long before DNA testing became available.

The Process of Palm Reading

Although each individual hand is different, all hands have specific lines and shapes that are examined during a palm reading. When a palmist conducts the reading, she first examines the six major lines of the palm, and then moves on to special markings, the five fingers and nails, and the fleshy mounts to uncover your characteristics and potential layer by layer.

Six Major Lines of the Palm

Each person's palm has six major lines, although these lines vary tremendously in their shape, texture, and length. These are the heart line, head line, life line, Mercury (health) line, Apollo (creativity) line, and Saturn (fate) line:

- The heart line can tell you about your emotional life, complete with your insecurities, fears, and passions. It also indicates potential for love or marriage and is sometimes incorrectly referred to as the marriage line.

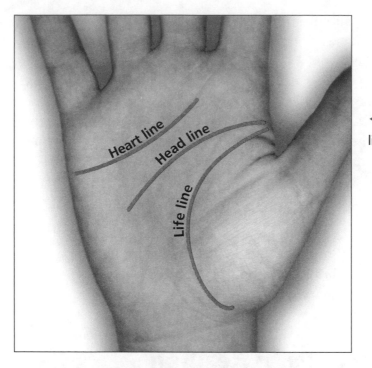

◀ Heart, head, and life line

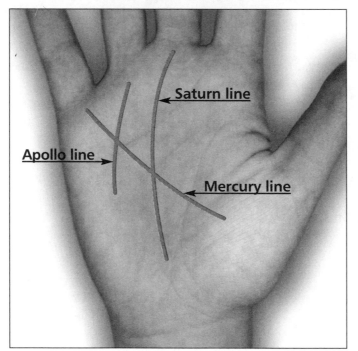

◀ Mercury, Apollo, and Saturn line

- The head line can provide you with a clearer picture of your mental abilities, career or business acumen, and potential for success.
- The life line is more than just an indicator of how long you will live. This line speaks to your personal longevity, stamina, and vitality.
- The Mercury line carries information about your health (and especially your central nervous system, which is the "messenger" system in your body). This line may also show your spirit of adventure and a healthy curiosity.
- The Apollo line demonstrates your potential for successful development of special talents, creativity, and life energies.
- The Saturn line is your fate line. It can tell you what fate has in store for you, and whether you are willing or able to accept the responsibilities that will come with whatever fate deals you in life.

ALERT!

Our hands have a language of their own. We use them to gesture, wave, and even communicate via sign language, but the most detailed information comes from reading the lines, patterns, and shapes of the hand. Still, you can tell a lot about a person just from his or her handshake.

Special Markings

Special hand markings that carry meaning in palmistry also vary quite a bit, and each marking has a particular interpretation that relates to a challenge or obstacle you may face. First, lines are examined in terms of their depth; then, the palm reader evaluates their unique characteristics. For instance, your life line could have several crosses or tassels around it; this is not an inherently bad thing but could definitely point to some major life obstacles you've had (or will have) to overcome.

Time is determined in specific increments along each line, and these imaginary markings (documented only on palmistry charts) could well be called "mile-markers along the highway of life." These, too, are not hard and fast—there could be a variance of a year or more in some areas of your life. The important thing is to realize that your opportunities in life come in increments or units of time rather than on specific dates. If you're looking for a reading that says you will find the perfect mate on Thursday, January 9, 2004, you won't find what you're seeking through palmistry. Rather, palmistry will tell you during which period of your life you have the greatest chance to find lasting love and happiness.

A Two-Handed Proposition

The overall size, shape, and texture of the hand are also taken into consideration during a palm reading. For instance, long, thin hands generally indicate that a person is creative and intuitive, while shorter, stubbier hands typically connote a hardworking or athletic type of person.

Both hands must be read to achieve the fullest picture of where you've been and where you're going in life. Your primary hand, and the first one to be read, is the one you use the most in your daily life (usually the one you write with). This hand will tell you how well you've been able to meet the challenges or opportunities presented in your minor hand. You'll notice lots of similarity between the hands, with slight to moderate variance on the lines.

Many palmists believe that as your mind undergoes changes, so do the lines on your palms. You should read your palms over a long period of time to record any changes that may occur.

Many of your mental or physical gifts are detailed on your minor hand, but not on your major one. This should not simply be interpreted as a failure to use your gifts to their fullest potential—it might just mean a missed opportunity, one of many to come.

Today's Palmists

The majority of palmists today read for fun, and to help others in developing a deeper understanding of their inner selves. People seek out palm readers when they want to know general things about their life, but also when they want to know specifics about why something did or did not work out the way they had planned. They want to know whether a true love really exists for them, and how or when they might be likely to get that raise or promotion. They want to know more about the causes, effects, and choices that affect every major aspect of their lives.

What's involved in a typical reading, and how can it help you to improve your life? A reading may cover a wide range of elements. For starters, there's the overall personality assessment, which gives you a fairly complete picture of your temperament, abilities, and challenges. But there's also a deeper assessment of your inner and outer health and well-being, coupled with a complete foretelling of your future. Some readers even claim to see the history of your past lives in the lines of your hand, although these lines more typically represent the patterns in this lifetime. Past life information usually isn't visible on the hand unless there is an important lesson carried from one life into the next.

Finding a Good Reader

Now that you know the history and modern uses of palm reading, you may feel ready to have your palms read by a professional. A palm reading could be a very special experience, if you find a professional palm reader who truly knows what he or she is doing. As you look for a palm reader, be aware that there are three types of palm readers out there: the expert, the novice, and the charlatan. While you may decide to visit the expert or the novice, you really do want to stay away from the charlatans!

The Expert

These are the folks who have been around for many years and who have done numerous readings, especially for people of note. While these readers can be quite accurate, they can also be very expensive—with some charging $100 or more for a simple palm reading!

If you have an immediate situation that requires the insights only a palm reader can offer, or if you have some extra cash and don't mind parting with it in exchange for a high-quality reading, go ahead and choose one of the experts.

E ALERT!

There are many palm readers and so-called advisors who are frauds, so don't just walk into any place that advertises palm readings. Your best bet is to talk to others who have sought psychic guidance through palm reading; check with the Better Business Bureau; or find a good reader through reputable sources, such as a metaphysical bookstore, society, or association.

The Novice

The second type of palm reader is one who is just starting out and is priced fairly but lacks the special skill to give you an in-depth reading. These novices can actually give decent readings, especially if you just want a fun overview of your life and future potential. Novices typically charge anywhere from $10 to $40 for a reading that lasts between fifteen and thirty minutes. More often than not, these readers can be found at local psychic fairs and in the phone book.

The Charlatan

The final category is made up of the people who pretend to be palm readers but who only skim the surface, offering few meaningful details and constantly asking for "donations" for candles, additional prayers, and the like. These readers charge a low amount to begin with, then hike up the cost by telling you that you have an "evil eye" or some kind of curse on you. Often, their services include a psychic laundry list of offerings; palmistry is just one of several things they want you to choose, tucked in between astrology, tarot, crystals, numerology, runes, and aura readings.

Another hallmark of the charlatans is that they typically read only one hand and only the three major lines (heart, head, and life). A good reader will look at all of your lines to give you a comprehensive look at your life, accomplishments, and potential.

A Rewarding Inner Journey

Although of course you may want to visit a professional palm reader, you can also do palm reading yourself, whether you read your own hands or the hands of others. Palm reading can be a richly rewarding experience along your path to in-depth personal understanding. Once you know what your personal challenges and opportunities are, you can better improve upon or capitalize on them to create a happier and more meaningful life. Reading the palms of others around you can greatly improve your communication. For instance, you can modify the way you communicate with an individual based on what you can guess about their personality, avoiding personality clashes before they become an issue.

QUESTION?

If I do a reading for myself, how accurate would it be?
Once you've learned everything you can about palmistry, you can quickly and easily do a self-reading. However, an in-depth reading does require the ability to separate your wishes from the reality of your hand. One way of creating some distance is to use an inkpad or photocopier to create prints of your hand, then doing a reading from the copy.

Learning the ways of ancient and modern palmistry can open up a whole new way of seeing the world. It can help you achieve the true potential you were born with in this life while helping others to improve their lives by seeing themselves as they really are.

You don't have to be a psychic medium to become a palmist—all you need is a wide-open mind and the willingness to be honest with yourself and others. Don't be afraid to look at the challenges realistically rather than tell yourself or others only the things you or they would most like to hear. Remember, the future is all about potential and choice, so there's nothing to be afraid of!

Now that you know you can effectively read your palms for yourself, why not set aside a quiet, meditative space for your first personal reading—or buddy up with a friend or family member to read each other's palms? If you feel ready to try a reading of your own, you're ready to move on to the next chapters. Ⓔ

Chapter 2

Take a Look at Your Hand

Before the palm reader looks at the lines on your palm, he or she will make careful observations about your hand—its shape, texture, and overall appearance. The information that may be gleaned from these observations can tell a lot about a person. In this chapter, you will learn how to interpret the symbolism behind various aspects of the hand.

Overall Appearance

Before taking a deeper look into the lines on the hand, you should always begin with an overall assessment of the hand itself. Hands come in a wide variety of shapes and sizes; to get a clear picture of the personality type you're dealing with, it's important to start with a good reading of the more general aspects of the hand's outward appearance.

You can learn a lot about a person just from a handshake. Sweaty palms indicate nervous tendencies; patches of blotchy skin signal circulatory problems. Some of these things are self-evident—in other words, you don't need to be a psychic to know that someone with sweaty palms is a nervous type.

Here are the main aspects of the hand you'll want to examine closely as you begin your palm reading:

- **Size.** In general, people with small hands tend to act quickly and perhaps impulsively; those with very small hands are generally free, independent-minded thinkers. On the other hand, those with larger hands tend to be more methodical and thoughtful about their big decisions in life. People with average hands are easygoing—they react according to each situation and its own unique circumstances and are not as predictable.
- **Color or consistency.** Color represents life or vitality. If the palms are pale—white, gray, or even bluish—there are definitely health challenges (most likely circulatory in nature); red hands mean you are quick to anger; yellow, jaundiced hands mean you have a pessimistic outlook; and pink hands mean you are well-balanced and have a healthy outlook.
- **Thickness.** Tilt the hand sideways and look at its width. Is it thin or thick? Thick hands belong to easygoing, noncompetitive people; thin hands belong to goal-oriented, driven, or ambitious people who are on a specific mission in life.
- **Texture.** Fine, soft skin indicates refined tastes and usually belongs

to the culturally or artistically inclined. Firm skin shows a healthy blend of physical and intellectual pursuits. Coarse, rough, or scaly skin indicates a more adventuresome, outdoorsy type for whom gloves (and personal well-being) are an afterthought.

- **Movement.** How does the hand move? Does it seem flexible? If it is, the person is also likely to be flexible in his or her thinking and general demeanor. A general rule of palmistry is that the stiffer the hand, the stiffer the demeanor. Have you ever noticed a person with hands so stiff they almost seem mechanical? People with hands this stiff typically have mental or emotional difficulties, or have a hard time trusting others.

ALERT!

At the start of your reading, you should always begin with a fresh, clean slate. Make sure your hands are free from dirt or debris, especially if you are photocopying your hands or doing a palm print using an ink roller.

Take notes about each of these items. As you get deeper into the lines, ridges, and mounts of the hand, you'll want to look back at your initial assessment to see how developed it's become.

Examining the Hand Spread

The spread of the hand tells you how you are perceived by others. When you turn your hands around so that the palms face outward, look closely at the spread of your fingers. Very close fingers connote a person who is very traditional and overly sensitive; fingers held further apart represent an unconventional, nontraditional thinker.

And what about the other fingers and their positioning on the hand? If all of your fingers lean toward the palm, you are possessive, reserved, and possibly even stingy. If they point outward toward the sky, you can be overly permissive and give until it hurts. A wider-than-usual gap between the thumb and first finger also connotes extreme generosity.

Look at your fourth (little) finger as it relates to your hand. Is it farther apart than the other fingers? Usually, a little finger that points outward and is spaced significantly apart from the third finger means that you have a quick temper and are not to be reckoned with when upset! If your index finger seems to be spaced farther apart from the other fingers on your hand, you have strong leadership potential and can be a trendsetter.

Hands that are very hairy on top can affirm masculinity in a man; a man whose hands are soft and free of hair often turn out to be meek and introverted. Women with more hair on their hands tend to be highly assertive and even aggressive at times, whereas women with smooth, hairless hands are of delicate constitution.

Your Hand's Shape

The general shape of your hand tells a palm reader a lot about your general character. The easiest way to get a quick read on someone is to look at the shape his or her hands form—and to correlate each shape with a particular personality type. In palmistry, there are four basic shapes and one hybrid or mixed shape.

Each type of hand represents one of four elements that the ancients believed composed all matter of our world: Conical hands are said to be "air" hands; pointed hands are "water" hands; spatulate hands are "fire" hands; and square hands are "earth" hands.

The Conical or Artistic Hand

Conical hands are round, sensual, and feminine in appearance. People with these hand shapes typically have a deep appreciation for the arts or, if the hands feature lots of curved lines, are artists or creators themselves. Quiet, sensitive, and imaginative, they are nonviolent people who seek solace through music, art, literature, and love. The conical hand is called the air hand, since this element most closely captures the free spirit of the type.

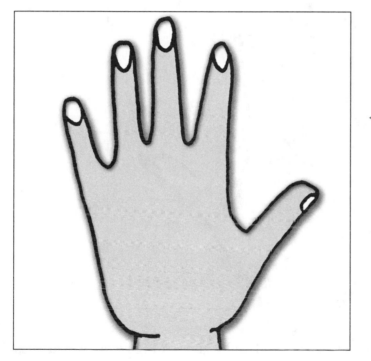

◀ Conical (air) hand

The Pointed or Psychic Hand

Long, delicate, and tapered fingers that characterize the pointed hand lead palmists to conclude that the fingers point to spiritual truths. This is why the pointed hand is always referred to as the psychic hand—and, in truth, the vast majority of those who have pointed hands do have psychic or intuitive ability.

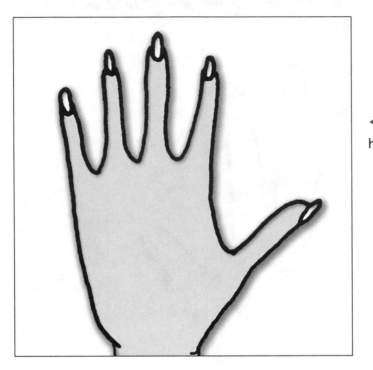

◀ Pointed (water) hand

If your hands are pointed and you don't think you are the least bit psychic, it could mean that you have the power but have chosen not to develop it at this point in your life. Whether or not you become a psychic practitioner in the future, your intuition and creative energy are already powerful, and you tend to have a tremendous amount of compassion or empathy for others. Pointed hands are often called water hands because of their deep sensitivity and intensity.

The Spatulate or Action-Oriented Hand

If your hand is narrow at the wrists, but wider toward the fingertips, you have what is called the spatulate hand. You are action-oriented and love unusual adventures; it's not unlike you to pack your bags and head to India for a spell, and then go on a skiing trip to Colorado the next month.

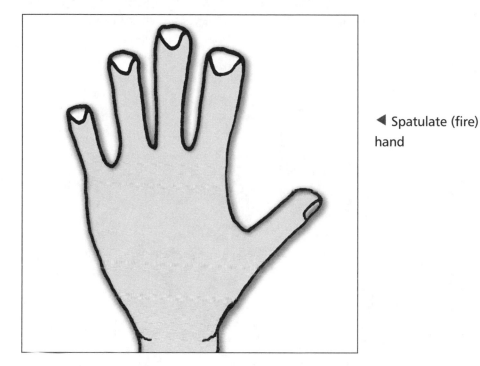

◀ Spatulate (fire) hand

An explorer of people, places, and ideas, you are daring, energetic, and fearless, often challenging the ideas or positions of others who aren't as open-minded as you. Your energy is boundless; you tend to leave others breathless, unable to catch up with you. Spatulate hands are often called fire hands, since that element most closely captures the personality traits of vitality and dynamism.

The Square or Practical Hand

A square hand appears to form a perfect square from the finger bases to the wrists. People with square hands are smooth, easygoing types who are very practical in nature and have a realistic outlook on life. They are rooted in their daily lives, and while they are friendly and outgoing, they also have a tendency to evaluate every situation as black or white, with very little left to interpretation. Still, because they are so sensible and level-headed, family and friends regularly seek them out to help mediate or settle volatile situations.

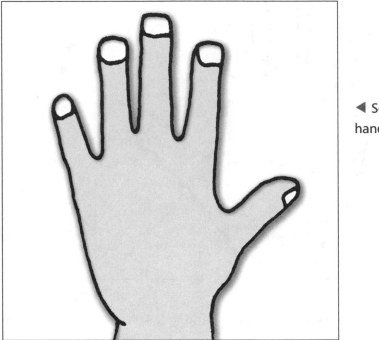

◀ Square (earth) hand

Square-handed people are most often drawn to careers that require hard work and persistence, since they excel in tackling large and difficult projects. Because they are practical and down-to-earth, these people are said to have "earth" hands. With the square-handed, what you see is what you get!

The Mixed Hand

Although it's quite a rarity, every once in a while you'll see a hand that has elements of two or more of the five shapes and types. Palmists call these hands mixed. For an accurate reading of a mixed hand, you'll need to look for the dominant feature of the hand.

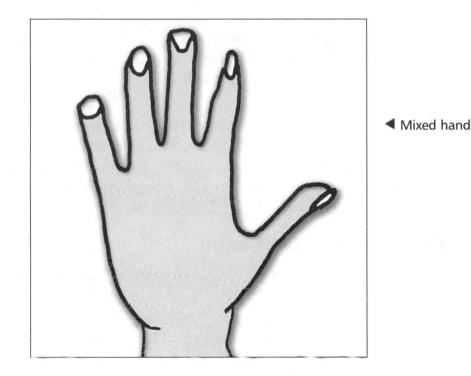

◀ Mixed hand

For instance, if you see that the palm itself is basically square but the fingers are long, it could mean that the person seems by outward appearance to be dreamy and intuitive, but that inwardly he is actually strong, practical, and even-minded. If all seems balanced in the hand, your mixed-hand person is completely versatile and has a steady, go-with-the-flow kind of attitude. Both temperaments have their positive and negative sides, but there is much to learn from the mixed-hand balanced individual.

Knuckles and Angles

Now, make a fist and look closely at the ridges that your knuckles make when your fist is closed. Do you see lots of peaks? A full "mountain range" with peaks and valleys shows a person who has good health, is adventuresome, and fights for his or her beliefs.

ALERT!

Remember, if you are right-handed, the right hand represents life as it is and the left represents your potential. Naturally, the opposite is true if you are left-handed!

If your knuckles are smooth and even, you are intuitive, impulsive, and dreamy. If they are knotty and rough-looking or heavily ridged, you are extremely decisive and not easily swayed by hard-luck stories. Tiny bumps on the knuckles connote a shy, introverted personality.

Inspecting the Palm Lines

Once you've examined the general shape of the hand, take a look at the palm. The first things you should notice are the main lines. Lines basically come in four different varieties: deep, clear, faint, or broken.

Deep lines indicate a person who is full of life and who is certain or direct about their needs and desires. These people have absolutely no difficulty in attaining their goals in life—and they don't let anyone or anything get in their way!

Clear, easy-to-read lines that are plain to see but not exceptionally deep typically belong to peace-loving, even-tempered people. These individuals are often the peacemakers in their families, and others look to them for their fair and objective insights.

People with faint lines often have lots of nagging health problems caused by years of worry or indecision. Often timid and reserved, these people would rather have others lead them in particular situations; they hate having to take action, especially for their own well-being—they prefer having someone else take care of them.

Broken lines indicate abrupt or traumatic changes in life. A broken line coming off the life line can mean a major shift in lifestyle or personal well-being. A broken line off the heart line may mean a dramatic change in relationship status, such as divorce or separation.

Long lines on the palm mean that you have well-developed interests and pursue them with a passion, while short lines generally mean that you have many different interests and can be intensely involved with each one—until the next opportunity presents itself.

Horizontal lines on the palm generally mean conflict or separation, while vertical lines point to a tendency toward people pleasing. Double lines mean that you have spiritual guidance in the form of an ancestral spirit, spirit guide, or angel—and this guidance pertains to the area of your life that the double lines are closest to (either heart, head, or life line).

While not completely conclusive until the rest of the palm reading has been complete, palm lines can tell you a lot about the basis or foundation of your life.

Palm Marks and Patterns

In addition to major lines, the palm contains lots of smaller lines and other markings. There may be tiny crisscrossed lines, loops, and other lovely little patterns. No matter how incidental these shapes and patterns may seem, your hands have carried all of these markings since about the third month of fetal development inside your mother's womb.

A General Overview

First, take a look at the overall texture of the palm in order to get a suitable starting point for reading the ridges and patterns contained in the palm. If the ridges in your palm are smooth and soft to the touch, you likely have refined tastes and are the quiet and sensitive type. If your ridges are wider and deeper, creating a rougher texture, you are athletic, action-oriented, and sharper psychologically because of your positive, outgoing attitude.

While it's possible for your hand to have no visible patterns, most hands have at least one type of pattern and a high percentage of hands have several.

The study of the finely carved lines and patterns in the palm is known as "dermatoglyphics." Here, you are specifically looking for the meaning behind each row of ridges and patterns etched into the palm of your hand by heredity, time, and experience.

Look for Shapes in the Patterns

Now that you have a good sense of the feel and texture of your palm, take a deeper look at the skin patterns on it. Do they form any particular shapes?

There are thirteen basic markings that can appear on the palm of the hand, and each has a special meaning:

1. *Chains:* Someone who is "bound" by worry.
2. *Islands:* Loss through difficulty or challenge.
3. *Dots:* Indication of a surprise or a shocking event.
4. *Branches:* Rising branches are a sign of good fortune; branches falling toward the wrist are a sign of potential failure.
5. *Broken lines:* A shift or change in life, or an inability to see things through.
6. *Forks:* Choices pertaining to whichever major line is closest (heart, head, or life).
7. *Circles:* Usually, circles predict great fame and fortune; however, you will rarely encounter them.
8. *Triangles:* Portend great psychic or spiritual abilities.
9. *Squares:* Ability to teach, motivate, or inspire others.
10. *Crosses:* Obstacles or blockages on the way; burdens that may hold you back from achieving your dreams.
11. *Tassels:* Not typically seen on the hand; can represent scattered energies or unmanifested ideas.
12. *Grilles:* Represent lots of starting and stopping with respect to life's endeavors.
13. *Stars:* The most auspicious markings on the palm; people with stars usually achieve tremendous fame—or lasting notoriety.

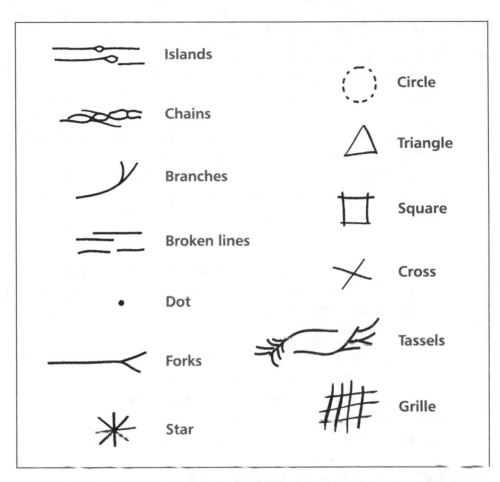

▲ Typical markings on the palm include islands, chains, branches, broken lines, dots, forks, stars, circles, triangles, squares, crosses, tassels, and grilles.

QUESTION?

Can ridges or patterns change over time?
They can, and often do. If you look at hand prints that are ten years apart, you'll see slight variations in the lines as the person has grown or evolved emotionally—proof that you can change your destiny!

Pay Attention to Loops

Loops are typically found on the webbing between fingers and on finger mounts (the puffy underside of the knuckles of your hand). Loops of vocation or career, found between the ring and the middle finger, show how dedicated you are to your career. If they are large and open, you are probably open to others' input. If small and refined, you are likely an entrepreneurial spirit who prefers solitary work.

Loops of bravery or courage are found just above the joint area of the thumb, near the thumb webbing. If you have one of these, you are fearless in your life's pursuits.

FACT

Check your hand for the "crowd factor." If there are lots of lines and patterns crowded together, it means you have an active imagination and like to learn. Having fewer lines is a sign of a more evolved soul.

Loops of humor or good cheer occur between the index and middle finger and point to a healthy sense of humor that draws others to you, while a loop on the Luna mount (the outside part of the palm between the pinky and the wrist) shows a marked ability to communicate with animals and nature. For more on loops and how to identify them, see Chapter 7.

Shapes That Predict Creativity

If you have several skin ridge patterns that seem to flow into each other to form a triangular shape, that shape is your focal point for creative energy. If you have a "tri-radius" mark on your index finger mount, it typically means that you focus your creative energy on leadership; if it occurs near your third finger mount, you are much more intellectual.

Whorls (unusual circular skin patterns) are a good indication of future greatness in creative endeavors. If you are an artist, writer, or performer, check your palm for any unique markings such as a whorl of music (typically found on the Venus mount, which is the padded section near the thumb) or a whorl of Luna (on the Luna mount). These two whorls signal marked artistic intensity and talent, and are rare finds.

Add a Little Percussion

The one area of the palm we haven't covered yet can be found by turning the hand sideways and looking at the outside edge of the hand (the area between the wrist and the pinkie). This area is known as the percussion, and it is wide enough to span three major mounts of the hand.

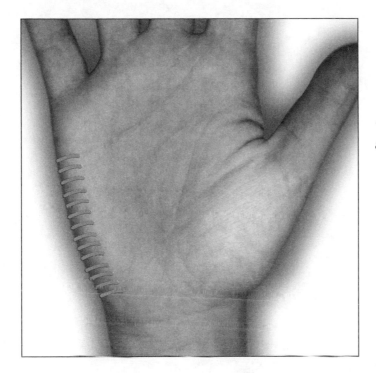

◀ The percussion area

When the percussion is tapered, it sticks out just below the little finger and then tapers off until it reaches the wrist. A person with a tapered percussion has an overly active mind and can often have a hard time relaxing and going with the flow. Curved percussions appear most often in persons who have lots of creative ability, though they may choose to use it in very practical professions such as engineering. Straight percussions are rare—they connote a person who is straightforward and who doesn't waste time on artistic pursuits. Ⓔ

Chapter 3
Mounts of the Palm

Y ou have already had a brief introduction to the mount of Luna and the mount of Venus. In fact, the palm is divided into nine mounts—raised or puffy sections that contain information about natural abilities, traits, or personal characteristics. If you want to know where a person's primary or dominant energies are directed, look for the most dominant raised area of his or her palm.

Hand Zoning

Before we delve into the mountainous terrain of your hand, let's spend a minute or two dividing up the hand into zones that will help you understand more clearly how each mount correlates with different aspects of your psyche and personality.

Hold your hand in front of you, palm facing the ceiling. Imagine a line that reaches from the center of your wrist to the middle finger, cutting the center of your hand in half. When divided this way, the section of the hand containing your thumb should contain zones that represent the conscious, and the section that contains the percussion side of the palm (near the pinky) represents the subconscious zones.

Many palmists add a middle "balance zone" to this method of energy division on the palm, because adding a third zone creates a buffer to allow you the flexibility in life to use the best of both your conscious and subconscious zones.

The conscious zone represents the energy that you actively use on a daily basis to achieve the things you want in life; the subconscious zone refers to the more passive energies (imagination, ingenuity, and creative thinking) that we unknowingly put to use in order to achieve our goals.

Horizontal Thirds

Another way of dividing your hand into zones is to split it into three parts horizontally (with two imaginary lines going from right to left), so that the three areas are the top (the area closest to your fingers), the bottom (the area closest to the wrist), and the middle.

The first zone, at the top closest to your fingers, is known as the emotional zone and represents your higher aspirations and goals in life. A highly developed emotional zone means that your approach to life is through your mind or intellect, since this area is close to your head line.

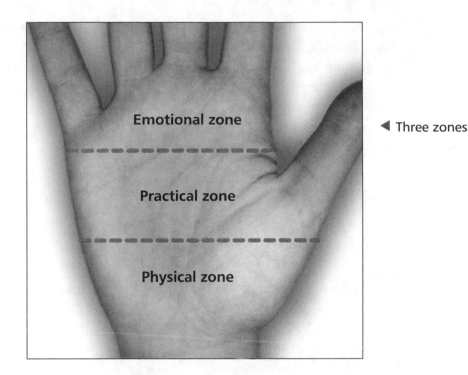

Emotional zone

◀ Three zones

Practical zone

Physical zone

FACT

The mounts of your palm can correlate with definite personality types as well as distinct physical characteristics; even though no two hands are alike, you will have much in common with others who share your palm mount type.

The area near your wrist is the physical zone, because it represents your physical needs and desires—and the physical energy you're willing to expend to satisfy them. An overdeveloped (puffy or large) physical zone means you will stop at nothing to get what you want—selfishly putting your own wants and needs over those of the important people in your life. An underdeveloped physical zone means you are passive and maybe even too weak to fight for what you want in life. If this is how yours appears, consider taking some assertiveness courses in order to better balance this tendency.

The middle zone is the practical one, because it is where the emotional and physical zones meet or converge. Check your practical zone to see how well you are able to balance the energies of the emotional and physical zones. If it's a firm, strong zone without a lot of mixed lines, you are adept at the balancing act—but if not, don't worry, since you are in the majority of people who are run by either their intellect or material pursuits.

A Four-Zone System

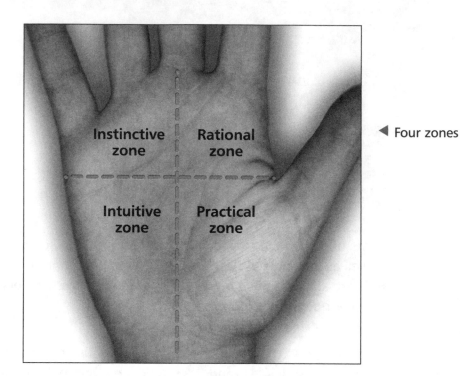

◀ Four zones

A mount that is less developed than others points to an energy force that is lacking in the individual's personality. Mounts that are overly developed show characteristics that are extremely noticeable in the person's attitude or demeanor.

Another zoning approach is to divide the palm mount areas into four equal zones or sections:

1. Rational zone includes your index and middle fingers and their mounts. When overly developed, this area indicates that you are a strong and ambitious leader; if not well developed, it can point to a lack of self-esteem or confidence.
2. Practical zone is the area that includes the mount of Venus—the puffy area of the palm that is connected with the thumb. Practical zone is ruled by the "pleasure principle"; people who have a predominant practical quadrant are into physical pleasure or creature comforts to the max. Conversely, those with an underdeveloped practical area tend to be unenthusiastic or even lazy.
3. Instinctive zone includes your last two fingers and their mounts. Many writers and artists have predominant instinctive areas on their palms; this is entirely appropriate, since this area represents creativity and communication. On the other hand, if your instinctive area isn't well developed or even noticeable, you likely have a difficult time getting your points across and may find you communicate better through figures, charts, or scientific study.
4. Intuitive zone includes the Lower Mars mount (the area underneath your index finger). A well-developed intuitive zone marks psychic powers and spirituality, as well as the gifts of humility and sensitivity. If the intuitive area isn't well developed, the individual could be atheistic and generally prefers an intellectual approach to matters of spiritual belief.

Peaks and Valleys of Personality

Whatever approach to zones you may choose, each zone contains one or more peaks and valleys. To examine them, raise your hand, palm up, to your eye level—you will notice that some areas of the palm stick up, some more distinctly than others. For instance, the cushion closest to your thumb may be especially puffy, or the cushion nearest your wrist might be more noticeable than the others on your hand.

Whatever the particulars on your own hand, you should know that in palmistry those cushionlike developments on the edges of your hand and near your fingers are called mounts. The interesting thing about mounts is that no matter what else changes in your life or in the actual lines on your hand, your mounts will not change. Even if you make a major shift in your career, love life, or personality, your mounts will be exactly as you see them at this moment.

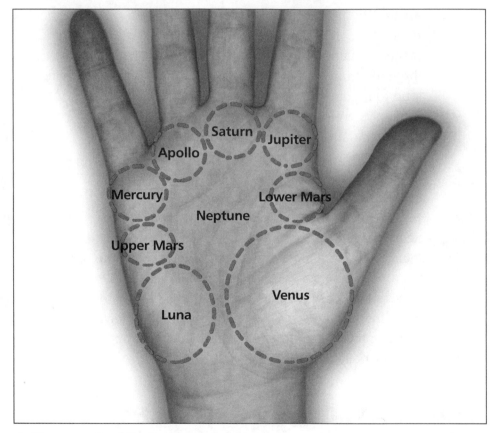

▲ Nine mounts of the hand

Your mounts represent the focus of particular energies in your life, and a dominant mount on either the palm or a finger (see Chapter 4) means that more of your energy is focused on that aspect of your life. The mounts of the palm correspond to planetary energies—each of which, not surprisingly, is associated with a particular character trait.

ALERT!

When reading the mounts of the palm, you should always read clockwise, beginning with the mount of Venus. This will help you to easily understand the nature of your emotional energies.

The Mount of Venus

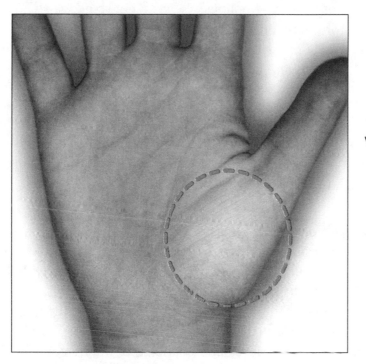

◀ The Mount of Venus

Because it is so closely associated with your capacity for love, affection, desire, and romance, the mount of Venus is the most popular area of scrutiny by a professional palm reader. When they have their palm read, most people want to know what kind of lover they are, who would be the perfect match for them, and other details pertaining to their love lives. The mount of Venus, which is located at the base of your thumb, can be a good indicator of how deeply or passionately you love others.

Tendency Toward Passion

If your mount of Venus is overly puffy, it can indicate a tendency toward promiscuity as well as fear of commitment. Just being aware of this tendency can go a long way toward averting its potential for negative consequences.

The exception to this rule is when the head line and the thumb are both strong and steady; in this case, your passionate nature will be tempered by a sound, moral ability to size up sexual situations for what they are—and to escape the emptiness of one-night stands. Instead, you will likely focus your passionate energies into providing a life of luxury and fulfillment for your perfect mate—turning your physical passions into material ones with real and achievable goals behind them.

ESSENTIAL

The mount of Venus represents love, home, family, sensuality, and morality, as well as passion in the form of emotions and physical energy. That is why the mount of Venus is also a window to your drive and zest for life.

Of course, love of material pleasures comes at a price: You might find that in your quest to provide a wonderful life for your spouse or significant other, you are less inclined to remember those sweet little gestures that keep the flames of love alive. If you find yourself overlooking romantic love, you need to work harder at keeping a balance between material and physical pleasures!

If you don't have a well-developed head line or thumb configuration, an exaggerated mount of Venus can indicate a callous, uncaring tendency toward instant gratification.

The Venus-Blessed

In general, people with a predominant mount of Venus fall into a physical type with round faces dominated by large "doelike" eyes and voluptuous lips, while other facial features tend to be smaller than average. They are usually slightly taller than other types, and most often have a very robust, healthy outlook on life. Venusians are, of course, the most sensual and socially outgoing of the mount types. They know how to live passionately—and well.

Do you have a love of the finer things in life? Is your home filled with lots of soft, sensual accessories mixed with very special works of art? Take a look at your mount of Venus—more than likely, you'll notice a predominant mount. Since they have such a keen understanding of human emotion, Venusians make excellent psychologists, teachers, and even politicians.

A Love of Luxury

A somewhat developed mount of Venus means you more than likely have a love of luxury and aesthetically pleasing things, so the way to your heart would be through pricey gifts. For you, truth and beauty are one and the same. You believe in love at first sight, and once you fall, you fall hard—and blind. You slip on the rose-colored glasses and see only the beauty in the object of your affections. Of course, if it doesn't wind up happily ever after for you, you might feel you were fooled by a "beautiful liar" and refuse to learn the lesson that all is seldom as it first seems. Though you are often advised to look beyond first impressions, it's not in your nature to do so, and you are often doomed to repeat mistakes in the affairs of the heart.

How can this situation be remedied? Well, you might get lucky and find a person who is physically attractive and is a person of strong character. If you do, you will have found your perfect match, since it will take a strong, honest, and attractive person to appeal to all of your senses.

Smooth Operator

What if your mount of Venus is not well developed? A nearly smooth Venus mount can indicate a calculating and overly critical disposition. For these types, beauty is almost offensive, since they are acutely aware that it is only skin-deep. Still, if you have other positive aspects to balance out your palm, you will probably be more of a kindhearted lover than a hot-and-heavy one. Is this a bad thing? No, especially when you consider that physical passion wanes after a time.

If your palm places you in this category, look for a partner whose mount of Venus is similar to yours; though opposites can attract, they don't always stay together for the long haul. A couple with small mounts of Venus can find lasting love together simply because neither sees physical passion as a requirement of the relationship.

What if my only noticeable mount is the mount of Venus?
While this is not common, it is entirely possible that your energies in all directions of your life are well balanced and that one does not dominate the other. You would make an excellent diplomat!

The Mounts of Mars

While Venus represents the forces of love and peace, the mounts of Mars represent the energies of aggression and courage. By examining these mounts, you can find out if a person's primary response to challenging situations is fight or flight.

There are actually two mounts associated with the action planet of Mars: the mount of Upper Mars (located on the outside area of your palm, just under your little finger) and the mount of Lower Mars (that area in-between your thumb and index finger).

Lower Mars shows your capacity for physical strength or endurance, while Upper Mars tells the story of your moral code. The mounts of Upper and Lower Mars are sometimes referred to as the mount of Mars Positive (Upper) and mount of Mars Negative (Lower).

FACT

In a perfectly balanced person, the two mounts of Mars are developed at the same level or to the same degree. Differing mounts of Mars indicate that you possess tremendous courage and conviction but aren't motivated to use them in a positive direction, or that you have the energy to act but little conviction or belief and therefore can't figure out which direction to take.

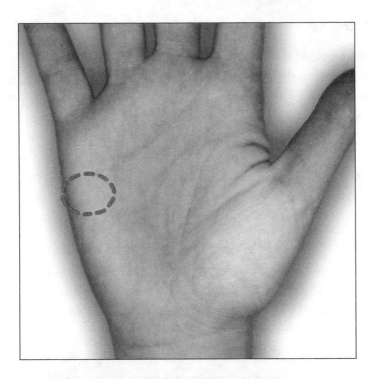

◄ The Mount of
Upper Mars

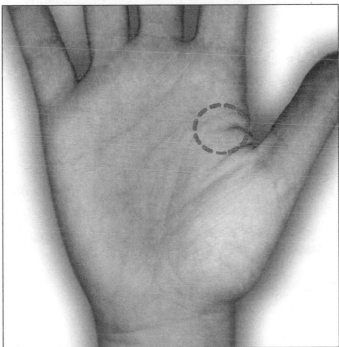

◄ The Mount of
Lower Mars

Life on Upper Mars

A well-developed mount of Upper Mars indicates that you are somewhat confrontational. Fortunately, that negative quality can be turned into a positive one when a crisis arises. And an overdeveloped mount of Upper Mars can mean that you are a bit of a bully—someone who uses physical force to get a point across. You are especially competitive when playing games or participating in sports. Watch out for this tendency—try meditation or yoga to balance this kind of negative energy, and remember that words can hurt as much as physical force.

If your mount of Upper Mars isn't well developed, you likely have a difficult time standing up for your rights; however, if it's the opposite—extremely well developed, you are likely the kind of person who is always ready to take up other people's causes and battles.

If the opposite is true and the Upper Mars mount is smooth or not well developed, you dislike confrontation and look for ways to escape stressful situations. Since your strategic and survival skills are superior, you are very good at defending others and can make an excellent defense attorney. Fighting injustice suits your personality and mount type well.

Life on Lower Mars

People with a mount of Lower Mars that isn't well developed tend to have a cowardly nature or simply be afraid of confrontation. This is not inherently a bad thing, but it could make you much more cautious or less assertive than you should be in certain situations. If, on the other hand, your Lower Mars mount is overdeveloped, you may have an overly confrontational and even combative personality. Ideally, your mount of Lower Mars is well developed and balanced.

If You Are Predominantly Martian

In general, hands sporting a predominant mount of Mars (whether Upper or Lower) can signal a personality type that's quite forceful and dominant in heated discussions—you wouldn't want to find yourself on the bad side of a Martian. Still, even if they are difficult people when they are challenged or frightened, Martians can be fun-loving individuals. Martian types love to engage in lengthy discussions about any hot topic of the day, and are usually intelligent and social.

Martians typically do well in business and commerce; however, those with predominant upper mounts have an easier time climbing the ladder to success than their lower-mount counterparts. Physically, Martians are distinguished by their long, angular bone structure combined with a large mouth and a beaklike nose set between strong cheekbones.

Plain Talk about the Plain of Mars

In addition to looking at the mounts of Mars, you can also examine the so-called plain of Mars, which is located between the two Mars mounts, in the middle of the nine palm and finger mounts—in the very center of your palm.

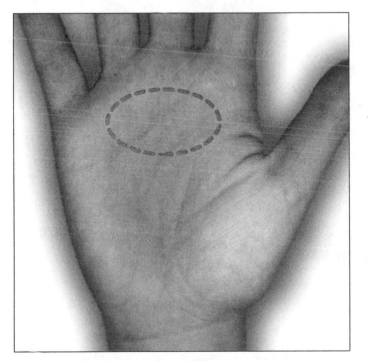

◀ The Plain of Mars

If your plain of Mars is thick and noticeable, you have a hot temper. If it's hollow and slight, you probably don't have the ability to carry across your ideas to others effectively. Of course, if your plain of Mars is not too thick and not too slight, you have a well-balanced temper and can see things clearly.

The Mount of Luna

The mount of Luna is symbolic of imagination, intuition, and creativity; it is located next to the percussion, directly across the hand from the mount of Venus. The normally developed mount of Luna shows a well-developed imagination and a passion for nature, travel, poetry, art, and literature.

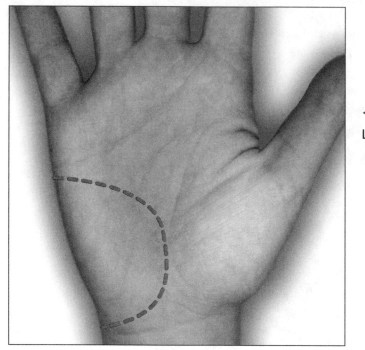

◀ The Mount of Luna

If your mount of Luna is overdeveloped, you might have some difficulty in dealing with reality because your imagination gets in the way. Check out your head line (see Chapter 5) to determine whether it is strong enough to handle your wild imagination—can it rope you back down to earth long enough to see the light about certain situations? Or is it too weak to have any equalizing effect on you?

If your Luna mount is underdeveloped, you are perhaps just as likely to process every new experience purely from a sensual, feeling standpoint—keeping logic and clear decision-making at bay.

E ALERT!

The ideal Luna mount is of average development—showing a healthy balance of imagination and reality. Individuals with an average Luna mount are definitely on terra firma.

If your mount of Luna is larger toward the wrist area (as opposed to near the thumb), you possess much in the way of intuitive power and can see well beyond the physical reality of life. You know things before they happen and are adept at planning your life accordingly.

Creative, Sharing Types

In general, people with strong Luna mounts on their hands are dreamy, imaginative, creative, and giving. They are very compassionate and helpful to others; often, they are quite protective of the people they care about. The Luna folks especially love to share their special creative gifts as writers, painters, or speakers. They make terrific psychics, artists, writers, or composers. And if a large Luna mount is coupled with a prominent Venus mount, the person is destined for world renown and acclaim.

Since the moon rules the tides, those with predominant Luna mounts love the water and anything associated with it. If you have this moon mount type, you probably live near the ocean or frequently travel there.

The Luna Hermit

If your mount of Luna is not well developed or is smooth or unnoticeable, you prefer to stay near home and have a tendency to live in your own little shell. If you do have any imagination, it's a secret that only your private diary will reveal!

Some readers include the mount of Neptune in their readings. Located in-between the mounts of Venus and Luna near the wrist, a thickly padded Neptune indicates charisma, while a deep crease shows an inability to look within for answers.

Notable Mount Marks

Mounts of the palm often display auspicious and/or inauspicious markings. Mount markings are cloudlike in the sense that they form symbols or pictures but may not be as perfectly formed as an artist's rendering. Although these same formations can occur all over the palm, it's important to note that, on the mounts of the palm, these marks have distinctly different meanings.

ALERT!

Just as you read the more general characteristics of the palm mounts in a clockwise manner, so you should do when reading the marks that occur on the mounts of your palm.

There are five main markings that typically occur on the mounts of the palm. Generally speaking, crosses and grilles represent negative signs, while stars can indicate good luck (especially with money) and squares lessen the impact of negative signs. A triangular mark on a mount of the palm shows wisdom.

Marking Venus

Let's begin with the Venus mount. Most often, grilles (mixed lines, both vertical and horizontal) that appear on this mount represent lots of misguided or splintering energy. Are you passionate about too many things? Grilles warn you that too many passions can lead to stress, tension, and an unhealthy intensity in your emotions. You will have to balance this energy with calming walks, meditation, or prayer—otherwise, you might be a heart attack waiting to happen!

Stars or Crosses on the Luna Mount

Not surprisingly, the star usually appears on the mount of Luna, and it carries with it a travel warning, as does a cross on the same mount. Be extra diligent when you travel; you can only let your guard down if the star or cross mark on your Luna mount is encased in a protective square marking.

◀ Stars and crosses on the Luna mount

Special Markings for Mars

On the mount of Lower Mars, the most common marking is the cross, and it signifies that you might have some adversaries out there seeking to do you harm. Could it be that they just want to undermine your credibility, or are they secretly plotting more drastic measures? Watch your back!

Of course, if you have the lucky triangle on the mount of Upper Mars, you will be able to outwit any potential adversary because you likely possess the skill to circumvent or diffuse any negative energy that is headed your way. Military or political strategists are often born with this lucky symbol on their Upper Mars mounts, as are athletes and salespeople.

On the plain of Mars, the most common symbol is the cross. Look carefully at your plain; since it often has so many lines moving in all kinds of directions, it might be hard to notice any particular symbol at first glance. If you do manage to spot a cross in this area of your hand, it means you are most likely very interested in studies such as alternative medicine, spirituality, or the occult.

Chapter 4

Mounts of the Fingers

Until now, we have not yet covered some of the most important mounts of your hand—the finger mounts, which lie just below your fingers. When you are doing an interpretation, it's important to first read the highs and the lows to see what areas are paramount in your life, where your interests lie, and where your talents and skills reside. After this, you should look at the lines and markings found in each particular area. Each star, cross, or square will tell you something about an area of your life that you need to know more about.

The Four Finger Mounts

In general, the mounts of the fingers represent the stores of energy that you have to dispose of regarding the particular attribute of that finger. A well-developed mount shows that you have a healthy amount of a particular quality as well as a healthy amount of interest in that area. An overdeveloped mount means that you may have too much of a particular attribute or too large a fascination with it. A flat or poorly developed mount means that you are lacking in a particular quality or that it holds little interest for you.

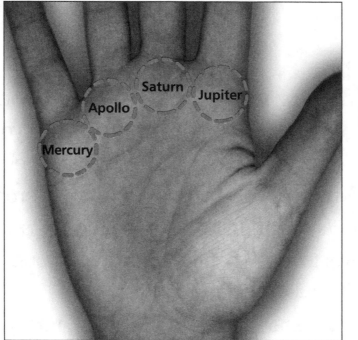

◀ The finger mounts

Actually, the mount of each finger is part of that finger, as you can see if you examine your hand closely. That is why we consider the finger mounts as a separate category from the mounts of the palm, discussed in the previous chapter. The mount of a finger will represent the same attributes as that finger does, but will tell you where that action takes place, whereas the finger tells you of your own temperament in that area and your portrayal of that characteristic in your life (covered further in Chapter 8).

Change and Growth with Experience

Of course, since your hand changes to reflect your life, these mounts will not remain the same size as you learn and develop new interests and respond to the different challenges life presents. It's fun to look at your own hand or that of a close, long-time friend to see how the lines and mounts of your hands have changed over time as you learn and grow.

> **ESSENTIAL**
>
> The mounts of the fingers are known by the same name as the finger they are under, and they are ruled by the same god—Jupiter, Saturn, Apollo, or Mercury. Thus, in interpretation, each mount shares the same qualities as the finger above it.

Reading the Mounts

First, look at the size of each mount. To tell if your mount is too small or too large, compare it to the other three finger mounts on the hand. The size of your mounts will be relative, with a slender hand showing smaller mounts overall than a large, fleshy one; so, you must be willing to judge a particular mount against the others. Slightly cup your hand and then look at it sideways from the wrist upward to the fingers to see if one of the mounts dominates your hand, or if it is smaller and your hand dips down in that area.

When you are trying to locate a mount, you can look to the whorls on the mounts to determine where the center of the mount is. It is not at all unusual for a mount to be off-center and not directly below the finger that it represents. The location of the mount in this regard is an important clue to the reading, as it means that the energy this mount represents will be skewed in a particular way.

A mount that is closer to the base of the finger shows an even greater manifestation in the hand of the attributes of that finger. For instance, the higher the Jupiter mount, the more the leadership potential.

The Mount of Jupiter

The area below your forefinger, also known as the Jupiter finger, is called the mount of Jupiter. Named after the Roman god who ruled all other gods, the finger of Jupiter represents the way in which you portray yourself to the outside world and the way you are perceived in that world. It shows your sense of self-esteem and your air of authority and control, as well as your idealism, sense of honor, courage, and nerve.

A Sense of Society and Justice

A well-defined Jupiter mount indicates a strong sense of justice and optimism, as well as charisma, outgoingness, skill in managing others, and ambition. A healthy Jupiter mount in a balanced hand shows a sense of justice and willingness to help others. However, if this mount is far higher than the others, it shows a sense of ambition to rule and the desire to control and dominate others, as well as inordinate pride and self-centeredness, perhaps even bigotry. Beware of greed, a need for power and arrogance.

If the mount is a widespread fleshy mass, but not a high one, it shows that you are an outward directed person, are interested in society and social activity, enjoy the company of others, and expect fair play and justice for all.

QUESTION?

Do twins have identical lines on their hands?
While they may share identical beginning lines near the mount of Jupiter, most twins have lines that appear slightly different from each other.

If your Jupiter mount is low or weak, it means that you lack ambition, self-confidence, and a social presence. You may be strong in body, but your personality will lack forcefulness. You may also just be diverting your leadership energy into too many areas, so that none of them gets the full attention needed for successful accomplishment.

A Veering Path

If your Jupiter mount veers somewhat toward the Saturn finger, you will lack the confidence to go it alone, and perhaps even the happiness of accomplishment; still, you will accomplish much, and with a more secure and safe foundation. You are more likely to cooperate with others, play by the rules, and to influence change from within rather than by redefining the world. And you will be driven by a need to make the world better for others rather than being motivated by personal ambition.

However, if the mount of Jupiter is skewed more toward the outside of the hand, you are more of an original thinker, and your visions for change will be based on fresh new concepts.

The Mount of Saturn

Your Saturn mount is located underneath your middle finger, also known as the finger of Saturn. The Saturn mount is named after the father of Jupiter, who was deposed by his son as ruler of the gods, but went on to found the Golden Era in Rome. Saturn is a symbol of success later in life, and his story is both a positive and a negative one.

FACT

Saturn generally rules the inwardly directed attributes, such as duty, responsibility, logic, and the acquisition of knowledge, rather than the outward attributes ruled by Jupiter. Saturn oversees all that went before you, the world structure you were born into, and physical and financial security. Saturn balances Jupiter's gregariousness and outward direction with a love for solitude, introspection, and self-awareness.

Depending on the Size of the Mount

Those with a predominant Saturn mount may be described as saturnine—gloomy and depressed. A person with too much of Saturn's influence will be too conservative, distrustful, rigid, and unwilling to bow to others. Too big a mount of Saturn means that you are too solitary, introverted, and aloof, too introspective and thoughtful. You may even become ungenerous and cynical, unable to trust anyone.

A level mount of Saturn offers a better prognosis—you are a friendly sort and think everything is for the best. You are independent enough to think for yourself, and you can balance trust and suspicion, new ideas and old values, the love of solitude and the love of friends. The person with a mid-sized mount of Saturn is one who exhibits just the right amount of common sense and responsibility without going overboard and becoming obsessive and moody. He is a leader in the sense of a manager or a company director, one who brings leadership qualities to an organization.

If you have too small a mount of Saturn, you lack Saturn's positive qualities: the need to look beneath the surface, the need to ponder and reflect, a sense of responsibility and organization, and the search for and love of wisdom. You may be flighty, irresponsible, disorganized, and superficial.

Off Center

A mount of Saturn that veers toward Jupiter shows a leader who is organized and thorough, having risen to a position of power slowly, by progressing through the system and by playing by the rules. A mount that veers toward the Apollo (or ring finger) side points to a leader who shines in a creative environment or someone whose art demands strict discipline. This person hopes to make the world a more beautiful place by balancing the aesthetic with the practical and disciplined.

The Mount of Apollo

The mount of Apollo, located at the base of the ring finger, rules those attributes given to Apollo, the Roman god of the sun who represents light and truth, poetry and art, healing and beauty. A good-sized Apollo mount means that you are outgoing and enthusiastic, talented and creative, lively and positive—a sunny and shining person. You are versatile, logical, and understanding, but your need to take the lead may sometimes make you unpopular. Your love for beauty, creativity, and self-expression may also be seen in your skills in crafts, cooking, and fashion, if not in the high arts, or at least by a deep interest in aesthetic subjects.

Too big a mount carries these things to extreme, and you become opinionated, affected, and loud, showing off your skills and possessions. You may care too much for the surface rather than the substance beneath it and become too impressed by position and fame. You may tend to overspend and burn your candle at both ends, maintaining a hedonistic lifestyle.

If your mount is too depressed, you may be dull, talentless, and insensitive to the finer things in life, willing to settle for a sterile existence; or, you may just lack energy due to illness. You hate being in the spotlight and are secretive, and you tend to cling to your in-group rather than face the outside world.

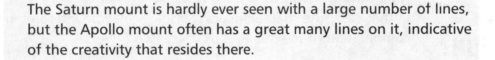

The Saturn mount is hardly ever seen with a large number of lines, but the Apollo mount often has a great many lines on it, indicative of the creativity that resides there.

Veering Off

If the mount of Apollo veers toward Saturn, you will still be creative, but in a less flamboyant way, perhaps as a writer of self-help books rather than romance novels. Your creativity may find a use in an area that requires staying on task and keeping organized, perhaps by creating an epic poem or compendium of world knowledge in one particular area.

A mount of Apollo that veers toward Mercury (under the pinkie) represents the business of art. Perhaps you will produce shows rather than act in them. Or your artistic side will find its outlet in communications. But in any case, you will use your artistic side to gain material success.

The Mount of Mercury

Mercury, the fastest of the gods, was their winged-foot messenger, and he ruled commerce and business. The mount at the base of the Mercury (small or pinky) finger controls your love for communication, expressiveness, and travel, as well as your abilities in business, teaching, and practical matters. Mercury also rules the sciences, healing arts, and even close relationships with friends and children.

A well-defined mount of Mercury shows that you are a speedy person with many interests, a good communicator, and a confidant. You are versatile and flexible, and you respond well in emergencies or when action is needed. You may make a good salesperson or businessperson, public speaker, or politician. You love family life, are skilled at number games, and are good at observation, so you can read others easily.

QUESTION?

What if a finger mount is not clearly at the base of any particular finger, but is between two of them?
In that case, the characteristics it displays may be interpreted as a combination of the qualities of those two fingers.

Development of the Mercury Mount

Too large a Mercury mount, and you talk too much, perhaps not always truthfully, and may use your gift to influence others wrongly. In any case, you will use your communications skills to advance in life.

On the other hand, a flat mount can mean you are a quiet or shy person, one who does not easily understand what is going on around you, or one who is too caught up in your life with little interest in others. It may be hard for you to communicate with a mate. You may also be impractical and confused. Many people with an underdeveloped mount of Mercury aren't successful in science or business.

Off Course

If the Mercury mount veers toward Apollo, look for an artist who understands the business of art, such as a gallery owner; someone who enjoys the little rituals of life and carrying them out graciously; or someone who has a strong sense of curiosity and many areas of interest. This person will be able to communicate creatively and approach any subject in a general way. If, on the other hand, your mount of Mercury veers toward the edge of the hand, you are the ultra-Mercury—fast-thinking, fast-talking, fast-acting, changeable, and totally into what you are doing.

The Lines of Family and Healing

In traditional palmistry, the Mercury mount is the place to look for relationship and child lines in traditional palmistry. Today, of course, we find evidence of relationships and children in other areas, such as the lines of affection or influence that reach the fate line (see Chapter 13). However, Mercury is the place where you can look to find out more about your familial relationships in general and your talent in social enterprises, which is strongly linked to your communicative nature.

ALERT!

We like to think that the lines that spring from the percussion across the mount of Mercury and travel alongside the heart line, formerly thought to indicate individual relationships, actually show your ability to bond with others and your propensity toward having and maintaining quality relationships.

Child Lines

The lines that run perpendicular to travel lines (see Chapters 10 and 17) are thought by some to represent the children that you will have, and some even think that the number of male and female children can be discerned in this part of the hand. However, others believe that these lines merely show your ability to relate to children, as a teacher or a coach or scout leader, if not as a parent. Indeed, a teaching nun could have a multitude of child lines. (For more on child lines, see Chapter 14.)

Healer's Marks on Mercury

In addition, Mercury, whose staff is thought to represent the staff of the healing arts, is the place to find the medical stigmata (see more about it in Chapter 15, which deals with careers). Furthermore, the mount of Mercury may contain Samaritan lines—five parallel lines on the Mercury mount are the mark of a professional healer, such as a physician or a nurse. If you have fewer lines, you might be a physical therapist or nursing home administrator, or you might just be very interested in health and the healing crafts.

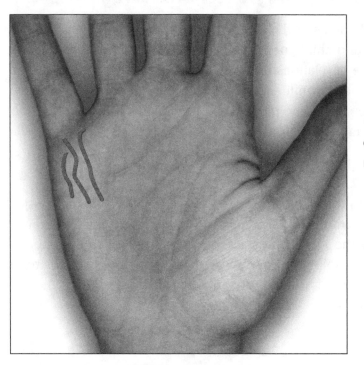

◀ Samaritan lines on the Mercury mount

The Basic Markings

Now that you understand the finger mounts and their significance, you can begin to look there for the markings that will give you further clues to the personality of the person whose hand you are reading.

The following are six basic marks that can appear on the mounts of the fingers.

1. The square is a positive sign that points to a protective force.
2. The grille signifies misspent energy and lack of focus in a particular area, so that the overall attributes of the mount are too strong and too poorly directed to be effective.
3. The triangle is a sign of success that results in forward movement and gain.
4. The star shows good fortune or victory, unless it appears on the mount of Saturn, where it is a warning of problems to come.
5. The cross generally shows a negative factor or opposition in a specific area signified by that mount.
6. A dot usually represents a health concern or another negative experience.

You may also find circles, a rare event, and lines that have specific readings when found on these mounts. One deep line may show success in the area controlled by the mount, but many lines can mean confusion.

These marks show a particular influence or quality; most finger mounts have more than one type of mark, so read the one that seems most dominant first.

Now that you have a general idea of what the markings of the mounts mean, you can apply them in specific areas to get very precise readings. Here is a rundown of what markings mean on particular mounts and in particular areas.

Markings on Jupiter

The markings on the Jupiter mount will give you more information about your status in the world and the forces that support it or diminish it.

- A square on the Jupiter mount relates to protection of goods and personal status and may signal the appearance of a person who acts as a protector. Many consider a square here the Teacher's Square, and those who have it make excellent teachers or instructors, whether it be in a school, the home, or in the workplace.

- A triangle shows success at the highest levels of ambition—as a world leader or diplomat.
- A star shows worldly or personal success won quickly and without too much struggle.
- A cross shows a romantic influence that supports prestige and position, perhaps marriage to the boss's daughter, but with true love at its center. Coupled with a star, it means that that person is a life partner.
- A grille shows that Jupiter has too much reign, and that the person will become too controlling and self-centered, trying for achievements with no substance behind them.
- A rising line means support; a double line on the mount means that the person is confused about which road to take to success; three lines may indicate total confusion in life.
- Since Jupiter controls the head, a dot can mean medical problems in the head, mouth, or eyes; if the dot is white, look for some kind of assistance in reaching your goals.

Markings on Saturn

Saturn reflects both responsibility and security, so markings here have to do with influences that will affect your property or your duty.

- A square means that you will own property or deal with it in some way; it also signals protection against financial ruin and security in career and the home, as well as in travel.
- A triangle shows that the person has an abundance of Saturn's love for research and study, and that there is an interest in the sciences or the psychic arts. Indeed, a triangle may signify a great deal of wisdom, inner peace, and psychic strength, which can help you in times of stress.
- A star warns of a dramatic event that may take place. If the star is high, look for problems with the law or society; if it is low, look for problems with your health, especially of the upper body's bones and nerves.

- A cross shows a sudden ending to a life event that will cause problems, which can be overcome with help from the positive aspects of your nature.
- The grille shows that the aspects of the mount are too strong, and the person becomes depressed and moody and may lose what he values most when old, perhaps through legal maneuverings.
- A dot that is black shows a loss of a parent or of that which gives you security. Also worry about health problems with your back or the nervous system.
- A circle shows that the solitary aspects of Saturn may lead to isolation; but it can also mean that the person will have protection and luck.

ALERT!

On Saturn, one line shows good luck, two lines show that you have the strength to overcome any bad luck; the more lines you have on your Saturn mount, the worse your luck will be.

Markings on Apollo

Because Apollo represents the arts and creativity, markings here relate to what you will do with your talents and abilities. However, they may also pertain to the lower part of the body, the generative area from which your life's creativity springs.

- A star here is a sign of success and prestige in the arts, with abundant talent and recognition of merit after much hard work. Too often, though, success in the arts can be bought at too high a price, and you must make sure you do not lose health, friends, and respect as you pursue your dreams.
- A circle shows success in general; it does not appear often.
- A triangle signals lasting success in the arts and the wisdom that comes hand and hand with it; it also marks those who go out of their way to help others.
- A square shows that the artistic reputation will remain strong and the audience loyal, and that artistic success will be joined to commercial success.

- A grille shows too much effort, wrongly directed, and in too many diverse areas. Any success will leads to conceit and smugness.
- A cross shows the end of the artistic dream, unless the Apollo line continues beyond it, in which case it shows a difficult life passage that will be overcome.
- A dot on the mount of Apollo is a very negative sign, especially if it's a dark one—it warns of losing favor with the world. A red dot means that your success may make you too temperamental, causing others to back away from you. In the physical sphere, look for problems with the lower body, reproductive system, and digestive system.
- One line means commercial success; two lines mean that while the person has talent, it may be misapplied so that success does not result. Many lines indicated even more talent, but they can mean that you have too many projects on hand. Horizontal lines block creative energy; a diagonal line running out of the Apollo line shows a deep interest in history and the past.

If a mark on the finger mount extends to the head line, its energy is more mental or intellectual in nature. Again, marks between two mounts are issues that involve more than one area of your life.

Markings on Mercury

Mercury represents many areas, including business, science, and communication; the legs and feet, which guide and propel this messenger god; travel in general; and familiar and social relationships. That means markings on the mount of Mercury can have many interpretations.

- A triangle represents commercial success and skill in politics and diplomacy, which rely on the ability to communicate.
- A square protects your mind from overworking and protects you as well from the damage caused by your tendency to say too much about the wrong topic to the wrong person without thinking it through. It also re-lates to business dealings that are conducted with honesty and fairness.

- Grilles can portend bad dealings in business, or else unfocused activity that leads to a lack of business success.
- A cross also signifies dishonesty, though this may be the kind of dishonesty that is needed by spies and actors—the ability to dissemble to gain a goal.
- A star multiplies the effect, indicating dishonesty in business matters, or it can portray skill and success in science or engineering (if the rest of the hand supports this interpretation).
- A dark dot can mean surgery on the feet, legs, or another area of the body.
- One very deep line shows scientific ability; many lines show interest in the healing arts.

ALERT!

It's easy to confuse the mounts of the fingers with the actual fingers themselves. To keep them straight, list them on a piece of paper when doing your reading   that way, you'll be sure to read them all properly.

A line on the mount of Mercury can also mean good financial luck—winning at gambling or an inheritance. More than one line can mean confusing communications, perhaps in a person too busy to focus on another and pick up the signals, or from mixed signals that cannot be read clearly.

Chapter 5

Three Major Lines of the Hand

Your palm's three major lines—life line, head line, and heart line—have a lot to tell you. They can demonstrate the talents and characteristics a person is born with and how she can bring these to the forefront in everyday activities to create the kind of life she desires. No one knows exactly how these lines are formed, but we do know that they represent far more than just the bending and stretching that our hands go through every day. They are created by the body chemistry in response to what we feel, think, and experience.

A Lifetime of Lines

The three major lines—the life, head, and heart lines, in that order—are formed even before you are born, and they change throughout your lives in response to stress and illness and according to your actions, which in turn create life changes.

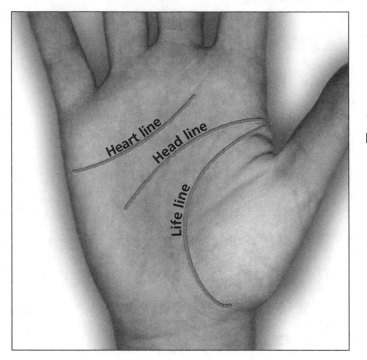

◀ Heart, head, and life line

As life goes on, additional lines will appear on your palms, and all these lines will continue to change and evolve as a reflection on your life and the choices you make. (For a discussion on these secondary lines, turn to Chapters 6 and 7.)

People differ in the number of lines they have on the hand, with office workers often having more lines than physical laborers, contradicting the argument that lines arise in the hand from doing manual work.

The Lines Themselves

When you begin the portion of your reading that deals with the three major lines, you should look at them in order of importance. The first thing to look at when reading any line is the depth and width. To get an optimum reading, the line should be even in depth and width. A deep line indicates a lot of energy and interest in the subject of the line; the stronger the line, the more important it will be in indicating what the person's life is all about.

In general, the more lines you have on your palm, the more sensitive you are, but an abundance of lines can also mean many possibilities and potentialities, perhaps too many to follow successfully.

The Life Line

The life line is the primary line of the hand, and everyone has one. As its name indicates, the life line depicts basic vitality and life force. It records physical being and warns of diseases, accidents, and other bodily events; additionally, it describes stamina, activity levels, and overall sense of liveliness.

The life line begins at the edge of the hand between the thumb and the Jupiter (index) finger and then arcs down around the mount of Venus to the wrist. You can time your life line to get a very rough idea of how long your life can be expected to last. However, such an estimation is also dependent on other factors, such as the lengths of the heart, head, and fate lines, so it's not a good idea to predict the length of life based on your life line alone. In fact, the end of life is so complicated a point, it should not be predicted at all.

A break or other negative mark on the line can mean any number of things, and making a prediction about the end of life can set up thoughts that lead to self-fulfilling prophecies. Think of the life line as showing you the quality—not length—of the life to come.

It's a good sign if the life lines on both hands are similar in length and shape. If the lines differ in length, you should pay more attention to the line on your dominant hand (the one that you write with).

Breaks indicate big changes and a change of direction such as a divorce or job change. An overlapped break means a change you initiated, while a clean break shows one that originated from outside. If the break occurs in both hands, the crisis is more serious.

Physical Condition

A long and clear line shows you have a good physical condition, good health, and the ability to overcome disease and injury. Your physical resources will be at your peak, and you'll be able to meet life's challenges with a survivor's instinct. Similarly, a life line that forks at the base of the hand shows that the owner is healthy and strong and can resist illness.

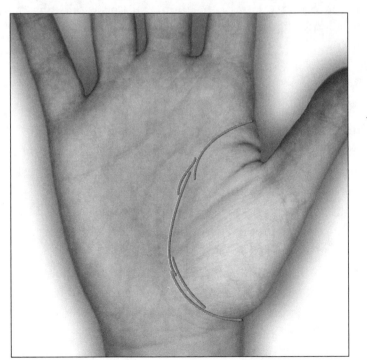

◀ A thick life line

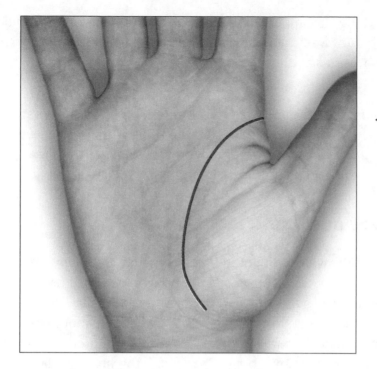

◀ A faint life line

A thick life line means that you are a very physical person and perhaps a violent one; a thin life line shows a weak constitution or personality, and perhaps a very sensitive and easily injured physical body. If the line varies in thickness, you will have healthy and unhealthy periods. If the line is reddened and deeper, the life may be an energetic and intense one, but this may be seen in aggression and hostility.

Begin at the Beginning

Be very careful to assess the true beginning of the life line. If it is chained or islanded at the very start, it indicates that there is some mystery about the person's birth. Any of the other markings found at the beginning of the line would refer to the birth as well. For instance, a cross is a mark of injury or distressed birth; a square is a sign that a certain problem was overcome and the child was born healthy.

A life line that begins on the mount of Jupiter (the index finger mount) belongs to a person that seeks a lifestyle change based on ambition and the strong pursuit of his goals. If the line starts lower down at the thumb, however, the person is a homebody or resident of a small town who wants to stay there.

A short life line does not necessarily indicate a short life. First, look for a new section of the line further on after a break. This can mean a radical and positive change in life—a move to a new country, acquiring a fortune, or overcoming a disease.

Between Venus and Luna Mounts

If the line arcs widely around the Venus mount, that shows a warm and receptive person who enjoys others and who loves to travel and the adventure of meeting new people. If the life line sticks close to the mount, the person is cautious, and tends to love family members and friends better than strangers and to stay at home with them; it can also indicate family commitments to aged parents. If the line actually goes into the Venus mount, the person is cold and aloof. The closer the end of the life line is to the base of the Venus mount, the more the individual wants to end life safe at home, no matter how far he has traveled. An ending at the Luna mount shows a restless nature till the end.

A longer fork that goes toward both the Luna and Venus mounts shows that person is conflicted about travel issues, wanting both security and adventure. A tassel at the end of the life line means that the end of life will see a decline of strength and perhaps a handicapping illness, which can be thwarted with proper care.

Forward-Moving Life Lines

A life line that moves up toward the Saturn (middle-finger) mount shows that the person is working very hard to succeed, but may not, after all. If the line moves toward the Apollo (ring-finger) mount, fame and fortune are to be expected.

The life line may also send up branches toward the various mounts. A line that goes up to Jupiter (index finger) shows a major advance in education or other activity that lead to achievement. A line toward Saturn shows the acquisition or property or material security. A line toward Apollo indicates success and public recognition, as well as love and affection. One branch moving toward Mercury (small finger) shows success in a commercial or artistic venture. However, if any of these lines are stopped at the heart line, there will be heartache when the venture fails, and if the line stops at the head line, the venture failed due to problems with planning or judgment, the mental activities.

Finger mounts were explored in greater detail in Chapter 4. These are the mounts on the palm that connect with the four fingers. The Mercury mount is the finger mount for the small finger; the Apollo mount is the base of the ring finger; the Saturn mount connects with the middle finger; and the Jupiter mount is the mount of the index finger.

Twin Lines

The life line can also have a twin line that gives the person life energy and added protection at times of trouble. This runs inside the life line and is called the Mars line.

But if the twin line is strong enough, the life line is considered a dual line, and it means that the person has a double existence. He may be a twin, but he is more likely to have two diverging interests in life that are mutually exclusive.

Markings on the Life Line

These marks are standard ones that can occur on the life line. They can also be read on the head and heart lines, with some reinterpretation to account for that area of interest.

- Lines crossing the life line show worry in personal matters. Lines moving upward show progress and improvement in health matters.
- Small bars or dots across the life line show obstacles that vex us at a

certain time. These keep us from advancing unless we work hard to overcome them. Bars can also be known as trauma lines and signify an emotional upheaval of some kind. A series of fine bars can mean a sensitive nature rather than actual negative events.

- A cross shows a longer lasting problem on any line, including the heart and head lines. This can mean the loss of a job, accident or other distress, and a series of these in old age can show bad health or financial ruin.

- Islands mean that there is an area of frustration, with too many directions to explore and too few resources. They are difficult periods where physical energy is low and resistance is bad, but they can be gotten through with work and attention to maintaining strength. On a life line, an island can mean a chronic disease or other debilitating physical condition.

- A chain of islands on any line shows energy being wasted, with resulting confusion and lack of focus. On the life line, they show poor health or many accidents.

- A tassel, or several lines, at the end of a line means that the energy of the line is weakened. On a life line, it means ill health or weakness.

- A fork on a line shows a decision that must be made concerning life or career as opportunities present themselves, and a branch shows that there is a link to another area of the hand whose influence will come into play.

- A circle can mean optical problems when found on the life line, and two circles mean a more serious problem, such as blindness.

- A line dropping into the Venus mount from the life line can mean a loss such as a death in the family.

QUESTION?

Are you an introvert or extrovert?
A wide-ranging life line is thought by some to indicate that the person is extroverted and has a generous spirit, while a narrow and close life line shows a person that is less giving and more introverted.

The Head Line

You have two major lines that run horizontally across your palm. The lower one, which begins at the side of the hand above the thumb and travels across the palm to end in a fork, is your head line. Just as the other two major lines, the head line appears on the palms of almost every human being—its lack is thought to indicate severe mental illness.

The head line shows our mental and intellectual life, our psychological makeup, and our intuitive abilities. It can also shed light on emotional difficulties as they influence mental health, as well as the physical condition of the head in regard to such things as headaches. The head line does not show how smart you are, but it can tell the palm reader how you think and where your skills lie. A fork on the head line can mean that a person is conflicted by too many choices.

A long head line shows intelligence, a good memory, a questioning spirit, and flexibility of interests, as well as the ability to reason and think logically. A deep and strong line means you can focus on problems and have a good ability to concentrate.

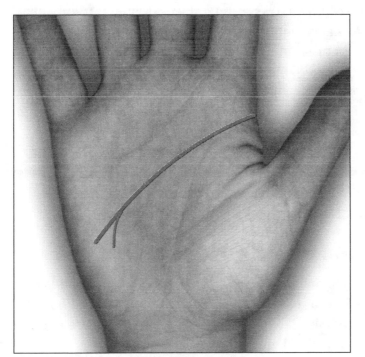

◀ A strong head line

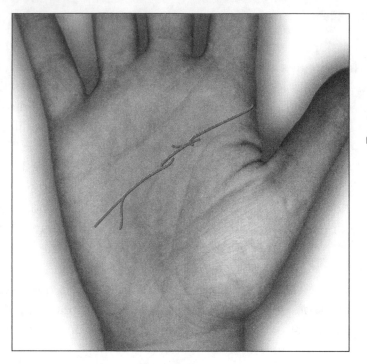

◀ A weak or frag-
mented head line

A short head line shows a mental world limited to practical matters with little imaginative flair, but it can also mean that your mental strengths are focused and concentrated in one area. The stronger the head line, the more focused you are, but a weak line shows inability to concentrate and a tendency to daydream. Those of you who have a weak head line may be indecisive and unrealistic, or lack common sense.

A wavy head line points to a person who is unsteady and unable to be trusted, and a fragmented head line shows a person who is worrisome, unfocused, or with a bad memory; he may also have a tendency toward having migraines.

The Straight and Narrow

A line straight across the hand shows an analytical and logical nature. Straight head lines are seen in the hands of pragmatists who are detail-oriented and organized, who can focus well, and who are interested in the sciences and technology.

A head line that descends shows more imaginative use of the brain power. An arched head line that veers at the top toward the Jupiter mount shows that the person will be determined to succeed.

A curved line takes a more experimental and intuitive approach, and creativity is seen in career choices such as writers, linguists, and the social sciences. A very curved head line that approaches the Luna mount means the person is imaginative and idealistic, perhaps a practitioner of the creative arts such as painting and poetry. However, too deep a curve into the Luna mount can signify an interest in the subconscious area of the brain or it can mean the person lives in a world of fantasies, fear, and melancholy, unable to interact well in the real world.

From Beginning to End

A head line that begins in the Jupiter mount shows a person with great potential for success; a head line that begins inside the life line on the Mars mount can mean an ultra sensitive and hostile person who likes to cause problems and cannot follow through when it comes to getting things done.

An island at the end means that the person may end life with a mental condition that is hurtful to those around him, and a slanted line at the end of the head line shows a person who is self-delusive and unrealistic.

Where the line ends is significant as well. A sloping head line that ends under the Apollo finger belongs to a person with many interests. A head line that ends below Mercury finger likes the arts and talking about them. A forked ending shows an analytical and persuasive talker, and a fork that goes down into the Luna mount indicates the ability to make an impartial judgment.

Branching Out

It is also important to look at the lines that branch off the head line. Rising branches bring good news. If the branch rises toward Jupiter, the good news will be academic in nature. If it rises toward Saturn, the news will be career-related. If the line rises toward Apollo, expect good news related to artistic or scientific success, or personal fulfillment. Finally, business-related success is indicated by a line that branches off toward the mount of Mercury.

A rising branch at the end of an island shows an end to worry. A falling branch shows sadness and mental anguish at that point in life. And a branch to the heart line shows a person who is cold and ruled more by his head than his heart in matters of love, or an unhappy affair that changes a person's life direction.

Special Circumstances Regarding the Head Line

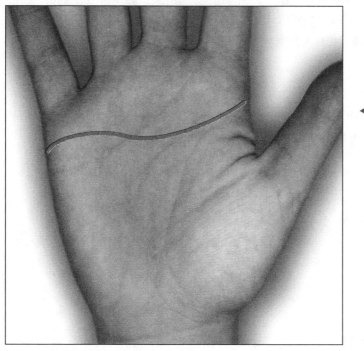

◀ Sydney line

There are also some very special circumstances regarding the head line that we must look at. One is the Sydney line, a head line that crosses the entire hand to the percussion. The Sydney line is not to be confused with a simian line, when the head and heart line are conjoined (see Chapter 7). People with a Sydney line have much in common with those who have a simian line. They may be hyperactive, commanding, and directed, but can also be self-centered and proprietary. They value the acquisition of money and are good at using their brains to do so, but perhaps not in the most honest of endeavors. They put work before their emotional needs.

The Double Header

A double head line is also very unusual, but if it is present, it indicates financial success. The person may have two careers that demand different skills, but work may make the person too busy and take him away from personal interactions. As with all double lines, the second line protects against problems seen on the main head line.

Markings on the Head Line

Look to the section on the life line for a thorough discussion of what markings on a major line can represent. However, there is some additional information you need to know in order to interpret special markings found specifically on the head line.

- A star can mean an injury to the head.
- Small lines that criss-cross the head line can mean worry or headache.
- A tassel indicates a weakening in the energy of the head line, and there is confusion and possible mental illness.
- Islands on the line show worry about work or money, headaches, and the inability to concentrate, especially if found on the Saturn mount.
- A fork on a head line signifies skill in business; if it appears on the Apollo mount, it may be a writer's fork, indicating skills as a writer.

A break on the head line is an event that results from a psychological cause or mental trauma. A square provides protection and an overlap recovery. If the break occurs below the Saturn mount, the hand belongs to a person who is reckless, clumsy, or prone to accidents.

The Heart Line

The heart line appears in the upper crease of the hand, traveling up from under the Mercury finger across the hand to an area between the Jupiter and Saturn mounts. Generally, it runs above and somewhat parallel to the head line, and it is present in almost everyone.

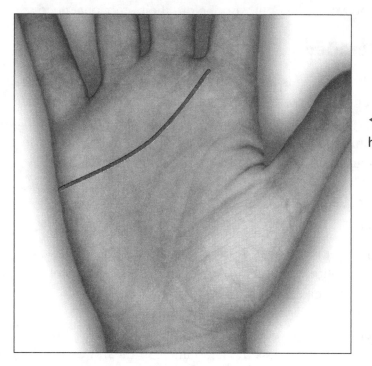

◀ A long, strong, heart line

The heart line gives an indication of a person's emotional life and emotional and physical relationships with others, as well as heart health. It shows contentment with life and feelings about affection, love, and sex, and it even indicates love for art and beauty.

In general, the shorter the heart line, the less likely the person is to be outgoing, while a longer line shows more openness and warmth overall. A heart line without branches shows a stunted emotional life.

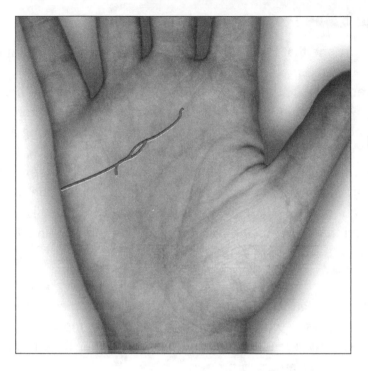

◀ A short faint
heart line

A strong and clear heart line shows generosity and a sense of
security about how others see you. A red or a darkened heart line shows
that you have a temperamental approach to life, be it passionate and
positive or hostile and negative, while a lighter heart line represents a
colder and more distant emotional state. A faint heart line shows that you
place little emphasis on emotional fulfillment.

Getting Physical

A curving heart line signifies a physical approach toward love, with
sexuality an important aspect of life. A straight heart line signals a more
cerebral approach to love, with more emphasis placed on fantasies and
romance. Those with curved lines want to demonstrate their feelings
physically and want to take the lead in physical matters. Those with a very
curved heart line find sex an essential part of life. Those with a straight line
need a partner who is like them in matters of the heart and mind, and they
base their romantic relationships on commonalities, care, and time.

How You Might See Relationships

A high heart line that turns upward on the palm belongs to someone who sees love in an emotional and romantic way, wanting lots of reassurance and a spiritual, idealistic approach to matters of the heart. Those with lower heart lines closer to the head line are more cerebral about love, and they tend to be less demanding and more giving and supportive.

The closer the heart line ends to Saturn, the more the person sees relationships from a physical perspective. If this line is short, the physical part of the relationship is all. If such is the case with you, it's likely that you avoid emotional bonding and prefer casual flings and one-night stands instead.

An ending between Jupiter and Saturn strikes a happier balance; it indicates a person who is reasonable about love and willing to demonstrate this love with deeds and actions rather than to talk about it and make empty promises.

On the other hand, a heart line that extends further, ending closer to Jupiter, shows an idealistic and emotional kind of love. An ending on the Jupiter mount shows a romantic soul that idealizes those it loves; when reality intrudes, these people can't handle it, and often suffer heartbreak. Endings higher up on the Jupiter finger belong to the hands of those who seek perfection in a mate. A heart line that reaches the Jupiter mount and then drops to the head line shows bad decision-making when choosing a lover.

Someone with a double heart line will be very loyal and faithful to his friends and will have added protection against any problems indicated on the main heart line.

Branches off the Heart Line

Downward branches of the heart line warn of unhappy love affairs or close friendships that end badly. If a line descends to cross the fate line, the person may lose their spouse. But branches that shoot upward signify good and positive relationships. And if your heart line has a shoot toward Mercury, you can look forward to well-earned financial success.

Often, the branches appear at the end of the heart line, where they signal diversity in terms of emotional life. Forks are common here as well. A double-forked ending shows that your life combines romance with practicality, while a triple fork indicates that your mind, heart, and energy are all in balance.

More Serious Problems

A heart line that enters the bottom of the Jupiter finger at its end is a very serious indication of major problems in life. If your heart line ends with a dip to the head line, you are likely to be dominated by the person you love and to give in to demands and jealousy. If this dip occurs below Saturn, the love will be all-powerful and tragic. If the heart line dips to actually touch the life line, you may be in danger of sudden death (though, of course, predicting death is extremely tricky).

FACT

If all three forked branches end in the Jupiter mount, you life will be blessed with financial success, happiness, and esteem. But if the fork splits into two the end of the line so that one end goes to the Jupiter mount and the other toward the life line, you will be likely to be misled in matters of love and romance.

A heart line that crosses the hand while a head line is still present indicates a perfectionist who is very sensitive and moody and ruled by passion, leading to jealousy, possessiveness, and resentment. If there are no other lines off it, a very unusual indication, it shows a person who is insensitive to others and who would sacrifice his family for his own good.

Markings on the Heart Line

Review the markings described in the section about the life line—the same interpretations will apply to markings you see on the heart line (or head line, for that matter). Additionally, here are some interpretations that are specific to the heart line:

- An island is a sign of an illegitimate or duplicitous love affair, but if is occurs below the Apollo mount, go see an eye doctor.
- A chained heart line with many islands shows a person who wants personal contact but is easily hurt and fears rejection. If you have a chained heart line, you are insecure and may fall in love too easily and too often. It can also indicate a health problem in the coronary systems and a nutritional or mineral deficiency.
- Breaks are emotional problems and warn about rejection, deceit, or unrequited love. Many breaks can means that you have the potential for repeated infidelity.
- A cross can represent potential for a coronary illness or a crisis.
- A tassel at the end of a heart line means that the energy of the line is weakened and relationships are bad or lacking.
- A circle on the heart line refers to coronary problems.

A branch off the life line can mean an adoption or new family member joining the household. A branch that moves toward the Luna mount refers to a traveling experience.

Relating the Three Main Lines

Not only is it important to look at each of the three major lines as an individual entity, you should also see how they relate to each other. First, check to see which of the three is the strongest. If it's your life line, you will value physical pursuits above intellectual matters. If the heart line is strongest, you may be impulsive and tend to place a greater emphasis on relationships and the emotional life. A stronger head line will make mental activities your favorite. It is said that a strong head line can overcome deficiencies in the heart line.

The Relationship of Head and Life Lines

The life line will generally originate in the same place as the head line. This is because the early part of your life will be controlled by your family, and your intellect has its origins there as well. The place where the lines separate show where the person leaves the family to venture out on his own and to think independently.

If, as is usual, your life line is connected to the head line at the very beginning, your hand will show that you have learned well in the family setting to be cautious and not to rush to decisions. However, if the two lines stay joined too long, you may have been too influenced by your family and lack an independent nature, relying on others to think for you.

If your life and head lines do not originate together and indeed they never meet, you may be self-reliant and outgoing—or reckless and hasty. If the two lines stay close together even after breaking apart, you will remain an independent and confident person, but a head and life line that are far apart show a tendency toward extreme impulsiveness and an inability to stay on task.

One Heart, One Mind?

A heart line that drops to meet the life and head lines shows a person torn between the head and the heart—one who loves mankind, perhaps, but can't stand people. But if the lines meet on a more equal basis, it shows the person can balance the emotional and intellectual aspects of life. Too wide a space between the heart and head lines shows an extroverted, tolerant, and original thinker; a narrow space shows an introspective and private person at best and a narrow-minded and a judgmental person at worst.

FACT

Check the timing of events or situations by looking at what is happening at the same time on other lines. This will help you to better interpret what is going on in any particular area, as all life events will have an effect on each other and help to modify or accentuate another.

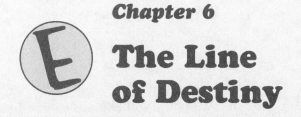

Chapter 6

The Line of Destiny

The line of destiny has many names: most commonly the fate line, but also the Saturn line, career line, line of luck, line of achievement, or the life task line. Generally, this line begins at the bottom of the palm and ends at the Saturn mount (the finger mount underneath your middle finger). Because Saturn is the ruler of duty, work, and security, it is indicative of the role career and responsibility will play in a person's life. Palmists look to the fate line to determine the direction of life, your control over it, and the ambition to achieve your goals.

A Hand for Success and Happiness

Remember that success is relevant—a remunerative and powerful position in life is not the same as a life that is happy and successful. Your fate line may show your life as unsatisfactory if you are an unhappy and unfulfilled senator; or, you may have a line that shows you as supremely successful, even if you are a dedicated clerk who enjoys the work.

Destiny Foretold

Destiny is something that we create for ourselves, and our destiny lines are mirrors of the efforts that we put into making our lives the way we want them to be. That is why your fate line can provide you with clues about your destiny and, in turn, can help guide you toward success and fulfillment.

In particular, your fate line carries information about your career, ambition, material well-being, personal success, and fulfillment of goals. It is the central element of the hand and adds stability to the rest of the lines because it connects the intuitive and the practical sides of the hand. It shows how you act, how you use your abilities, and how you control your environment and deal with its influences.

ESSENTIAL

The fate line also has another role to play—it shows relationships that affect our lives. Relationships are seen in the lines of influence that rise up from the mount of Luna to meet the fate line, and they can be marriages, important friendships, and business partnerships. (Lines of influence are any lines that run parallel or across major lines.)

Where Destiny Begins

For most people, the fate line begins at the base of the hand at the first rascette, or the bracelet line at the wrist, and it travels upward to the mount of Saturn. This is the traditional ending for the fate line, and those who have it have a secure sense of direction and purpose. A long and clear line can mean a career with the same company throughout life.

The closer to the wrist the fate line begins, the earlier a person will begin to develop a sense of responsibility and duty. His life circumstances may demand this, but it will serve a valuable purpose later on as his career develops.

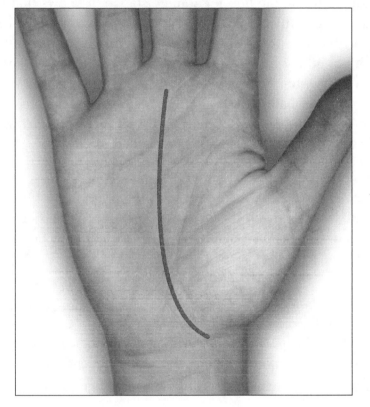

◀ The ideal fate line

A fate line that is long and strong signals an unusual sense of purpose and often belongs to those who go far in their careers. Such people have a strong sense of self and direction in life. However, a clear and consistent line running the length of the hand is rarer than you might think.

This is because fate lines can begin and end in a surprising number of places, and all have different meanings. In general, the closer to the rascette your line of destiny begins, the better. It means that you will learn a sense of responsibility early in life.

Family Business?

If your fate line in the mount of Venus inside the life line, it means you had help from your family when starting off in your career, or perhaps they were too influential in making your career decision. If your fate line is joined to the life line for some distance, it shows that your career perhaps began in a family business, that they contributed to your start in life, or that you are in some other way close to and indebted to them, though not in any negative way. However, where the life line and the fate line part is where you will achieve independence from your family on your career path. However, there may be light lines of attachment between the two lines that show a strong emotional bond between you and your family.

ALERT!

Be aware: A fate line that begins well inside the mount of Venus and the life line can mean that a person becomes enmeshed with his parents and the rest of the family and are unable to break away from their control.

If the fate line starts at the wrist and then veers to meet the life line later on, it means that your career development must be sacrificed to meet your family needs for the duration. In general, the greater the distance between the life line and the fate line, the greater the distance between the person and his family of origin, both geographically and emotionally.

Making Your Own Way

If your fate line begins near the life line but not within it, you will make your own way in life and determine your own priorities. Your success will rely on your ability to work and accomplish things for yourself with no outside influence.

If your fate line begins on the other side of the hand in the mount of Luna, which represents the social element, it means that your career will be in the public eye, as a politician or perhaps as an actor, but in some way that demands that you gain public approval in order to be considered a success. Your career might also be in the musical arts or in an area where you are dealing with the public (for instance, as a social worker); in any event, it will be in a field in which you are able to affect and influence others.

A Late Start

If your fate line does not begin until the middle of the hand in the plain of Mars, it may take you a long time to get started in life or to settle on a career and find your true calling. You will begin your career in struggle and uncertainty, but if your fate line reaches clearly to the Saturn mount, it will end in success based on lessons learned In the struggle.

An extreme example of getting a late start in life occurs when the fate line arises from the head line. This means your success will be gained through application of your intelligence and knowledge, but only later in life, as the head line lies so high up in the palm.

Sometimes a fate line arises out of a fork between the mounts of Luna and Venus, both of which influence the destiny of the person with such a line. Often, these people have a tendency to just let things happen rather than direct the course of their destiny. Worse, the duality that comes from a fork at Luna and Venus may lead to great confusion in terms of career, as work goals are continually re-examined and re-evaluated. However, if the line ends at Saturn, all will be well, despite the confusion and ambivalence.

The Shape of the Line

As with other lines, the shape and depth of the fate line is important. The heavier the line, the more independent and responsible the owner of the hand is—and the more resistant to change. A very heavy fate line can mean that the owner is stuck in too predictable a pattern.

It can also be an indication that this person pays too much attention to career goals while emotional, health, and intellectual interests are given short shrift. However, success in life is as dependent on these things as it is on hard work. Overall, though, a strong fate line is a positive thing, indicating that you are self-motivated, trustworthy, and strong. A deep line shows an ability to concentrate and an interest in the work itself.

A weak fate line shows a lack of direction and control, putting you at risk. A thin line of destiny shows a lack of commitment and stamina. And an irregular or fragmented line of destiny shows purposelessness, changeability, ill temper, and a person who is not in charge of one's own life.

What Happens at the End

The ending of the fate line is also of importance, for it will tell you a great deal about the eventual chance of a successful career. If the line ends beneath the Saturn finger, as is typical, security is of highest importance to you. A clean ending beneath the Saturn finger represents a good planned retirement. However, a forked or tasseled ending means a dissipation of energy and perhaps a less than positive retirement. Bars at the end of the line also mean obstacles and problems at the end of the career, and a danger of poverty and deprivation.

ESSENTIAL

Some people do not have a fate line, and this means either that their lives lack direction, purpose, and a sense of responsibility, or that they are out of sync with the prevailing mode of what constitutes success and want to make their own way through life. It can mean you are an adventurer, a wanderer who seeks a livelihood where he finds it.

If the fate line ends beneath the Jupiter mount, your lifework will give you high status and social standing, and you will have a brilliant career that fulfills your ambition, with power over others.

Moving Ahead

A fork or branch to the Apollo mount, or an ending of the fate line in that mount, is a sign of personal fulfillment in your career and artistic or intellectual success, usually with accompanying financial rewards. A similar fork or branch structure from the end of the fate line that ends near the Mercury mount means success in business or the sciences, or perhaps a special talent for persuasion and conversation.

Getting Off Track

However, a fate line that ends at the head line shows that your career is hampered by errors of judgment and intellectual missteps. And if your fate line ends short in a dead end at the heart line, your career may be sidetracked either by an emotional disruption, such as an affair at work, or perhaps by a heart condition.

If the heart line is deep and cuts through the fate line, interrupting it, it means that an emotional attachment has caused a financial fallback—this is often the sign of the death of a marriage partner that leaves the widow with too little income, or a deceased business partner without the insurance that will keep the company solvent. But if your heart line merges equally and gently with your fate line, you will have it all—love and affection, wealth, power, honor, and fame.

Attachments and Partners

The fate line is also a good place to look if you'd like to learn more about the companions that life will offer you. A line of influence or attachment can come up from the mount of Luna to join the fate line, and this signifies a business partnership or marriage. The lower the line joins the fate line, the earlier the relationship will be formed, and if it is a marriage, it is important that your career be successful enough at that time to be able to enter into such a life-altering arrangement.

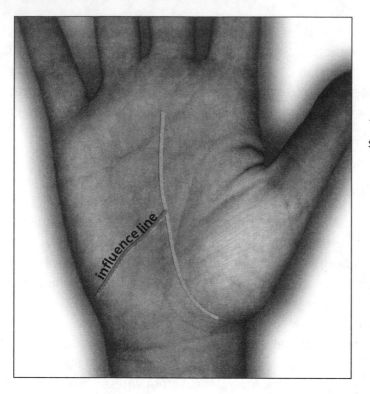

◀ Influence line may signal a marriage

If the line of influence is heavier than the fate line, the partner will dominate, but not necessarily to the detriment of the relationship. If the line of influence begins in an island, the union will bring misfortune to your career, and also possibly to your relationship.

A line from the Luna mount that does not reach the fate line represents a failed union. Furthermore, short lines shooting up from the fate line mean positive influences, but those shooting downward are negative influences.

Lines of influence can also arrive from the Venus mount, and this means the relationship originated in the family, rather than through the public arena.

Destiny Times Two

A double fate line can mean many things: a close business partnership or marriage that supports the career (perhaps in a dual career as farmers or entrepreneurs in a family business), especially if it begins on the Luna mount. However, a double line could also mean that you have simultaneously undertaken two disparate careers, sustained protection from career problems, or have enjoyed great success in a career.

A line that accompanies the fate line for a short time represents outside forces and interests that can affect the career, either supporting it or causing the owner of the hand additional pressure and responsibility by drawing his attention away from his career.

Markings on the Fate Line

Like the other lines, the markings on the fate line let us know more about what we have in store for us. Classic markings can take on new meanings when applied to the line of destiny. A short description on timing this difficult line follows.

ESSENTIAL

The fate line shows the degree to which we are successful at using our abilities and talents to realize our life's work and goals. It also records the challenges and rewards that we will meet along the way.

Typical Destiny Markings

A break in the line of destiny shows a change in job or career, and a sudden break is an unexpected change; an overlapping break means a change you controlled, so it might not have a negative outcome as an unexpected change would have. Many breaks signal many changes and the inability to take off in one direction in a career. A fate line that has many breaks, islands, and stops shows that a person has many changes of career or a series of unproductive jobs.

A short and light bar on the line is an obstacle that is short-term and may be gotten around with effort, such as a problem supervisor. If the bar is heavier than the fate line itself, it means a problem that is very disturbing to the owner of the hand. A series of bars can mean insurmountable obstacles.

A fork can suggest a change in career, or at the very least exploration of a new career path. Grille patterns with lines in both vertical and horizontal patterns can point to burdensome worries.

An island on the fate line shows trouble and frustration, dissatisfaction, or financial shortfalls. At the beginning of the fate line, an island can signify a mysterious origin, just as it can on the life line. This used to be thought of as a mark of illegitimacy or adoption, but now it is seen as a sign of some unknown influence at the beginning of life.

ESSENTIAL

A cross that appears next to the fate line may represent a crisis or change, but it can also be significant of something that will effect a positive change in the person's life by calling on untapped talents. It may cause a re-examination of old beliefs and a switch to new and more effective habits.

A cross on the fate line, if seen at the beginning of the line, can show the loss of a parent early in life. A cross farther along on the line means a crisis or a change in the person's life, and this crisis will have a lasting effect on that life.

A square on the fate line shows that you are protected from a problem. It can be a warning if it occurs in midlife to give the hand's owner a chance to prepare for problems, and it can also allow the owner of the hand to take a risk, knowing that he is somewhat protected.

A triangle between the fate and the life line signifies victory in military endeavors or at least winning a major battle if the owner of the hand is a civilian.

A star on the line of destiny is a sudden shock or disturbance in the career, a sudden rise in the energy field that causes a negative situation. If it happens early on the line, this could mean a familial emergency, such as a move or loss of fortune, that took place without warning but left emotional scars.

Timing the Fate Line

You can begin to determine when events will happen in your life as they affect the line of destiny by looking at the distance between the beginning of the line at the top rascette of your wrist and the natural end of the line, which is usually at the crease of the Saturn finger. Look for the midpoint between them, and consider that as representing forty years. If your fate line is shorter than this, make adjustments for your own particular hand. Then estimate, depending on the length of your hand, the years until your birth—the length of a year will vary depending on each particular hand, so it is hard to be more specific about how long a year's length should be.

Since some life events indicated on your fate line have already taken place, you will be able to judge which markings apply to which life events and make a fairly accurate scale of the years of your life. When you estimate the years after thirty-five, you should remember to shorten your scale to allow for the compacting forces of life, when time speeds up as it nears its end.

ALERT!

A fate line that extends beyond the mount of Saturn and ends in the bottom phalange of the Saturn finger is very unusual. It means a truly outstanding life and career, either in a positive or negative sense.

Determining Direction

By using this time line, you can read your fate line to interpret the direction your life will take and your confidence in achieving what you set out to do. When a reading of your line of destiny is combined with readings of the other major and minor lines of the hand, you will have better insights about how your talents and character can best be put to use in the public arena to meet your goals in life.

Chapter 7

Secondary Lines and Patterns

Once you have mastered the interpretation of the three major lines of the hand as well as the fate line, it is time to turn to some of the other markings of the palm. The secondary lines and patterns on your palm will allow you to understand a great deal more about yourself or about the person whose palm you are reading. These are usually not present on every hand, but when they are there, they will give you a much fuller picture.

Lines of Influence

Lines that run alongside the major lines of the hand are known as lines of influence. These lines take on a variety of meanings, which can best be explored by looking at the effect on the major line with which they merge. If the line of influence runs parallel with the line you are studying, it serves to strengthen that line at its weakest points, repairing a break or serving as a companion line in times of strife.

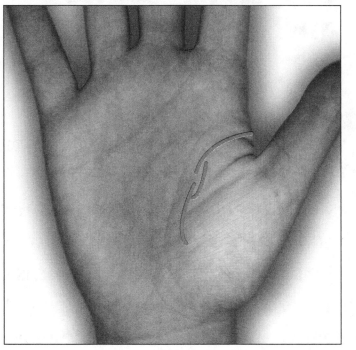

◀ Parallel lines of influence

Lines of influence that end in a star show that the influence is over. A line from a star at the end of a line of influence that cuts past the life line means that a close relative will die at about that time on the life line.

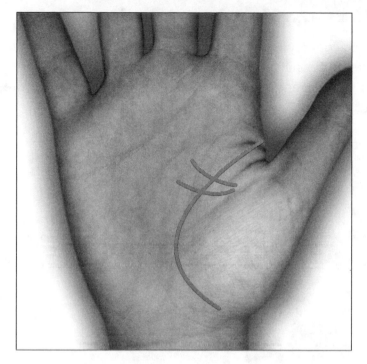

◀ Perpendicular
lines of influence

Lines that run perpendicular to another line usually serve to bar the path and show obstacles, problems, and trials. If these lines form a widened area like a dot, there will be a major problem, and you should look to see if the section following on the line indicates an island or break.

The Planet Lines

The three lines of influence that run vertically along the palm's length (from the wrist up to the fingers) are the Mercury line, Mars line, and Apollo line. They begin in the lower area of the palm, sometimes as far down as the wrist, and end at the top of the hand in or near the upper mounts below the fingers. These lines are named after the finger mount in which it has its ending. Here is how to read these lines.

The Line of Mercury: Health and Business Savvy

Of all the secondary lines, the Mercury line is the most often found among the general population. The line may begin on the mount of Luna or Venus (or in between the two) and generally runs upward to the mount of Mercury.

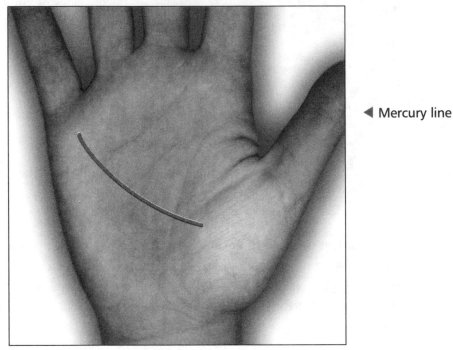

◀ Mercury line

A strong and deep Mercury line indicates good business sense. However, Mercury is generally known as a health line. In fact, at one time it was called the hepatica line, named from the Latin word for liver, because it was an indicator of poor health and especially of liver ailments.

The messenger god Mercury is often aligned with the Roman god of healing and medicine, Aesculapius (because Mercury's winged staff is similar to the entwined serpent staff of that god). If your Mercury line crosses the life line, you either have a deep interest in learning about health matters, you work in a health-care profession, or are involved in healing in some other way, be it spiritual or psychological.

If the Mercury line begins in the mount of Venus, you can use it to judge the state of your health. It gets deeper when one is in poor health or worn out and vulnerable, but decreases in prominence when health issues are addressed successfully. A Mercury line that is broken or chained shows periods of ill health, either for the owner of the palm or else for someone for whom the owner cares.

If the Mercury line begins in the mount of Luna or if it originates in the life line, you have the intuitiveness and insight to be successful in business or as a business leader.

The Line of Mars: Courage and Strength

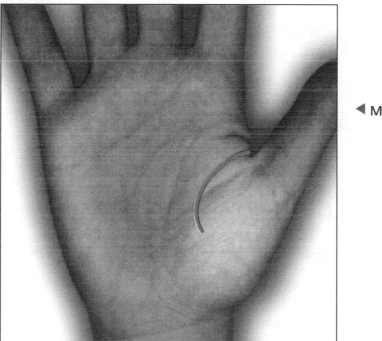

◀ Mars line

Mars is the god of war, and a line with his name will run alongside the life line on the thumb side. It may be short or long—in either case, its appearance indicates extra strength and protection to the person's life.

This is especially important if there are breaks or other weaknesses on the life line. The Mars line gives added energy and endurance so the person can overcome health problems that are seen on the life line. A Mars line can also symbolize a good strong friend that will stand up for you and aid you in times of trouble—a true companion and lifelong ally.

ALERT!

If the line of Mars ends on the Luna mount with a cross, star, or other very definitive ending, death may be the result of drug or alcohol abuse. If at the same time the head line ends in a star, expect a mental breakdown.

The Line of Apollo: The Success Line

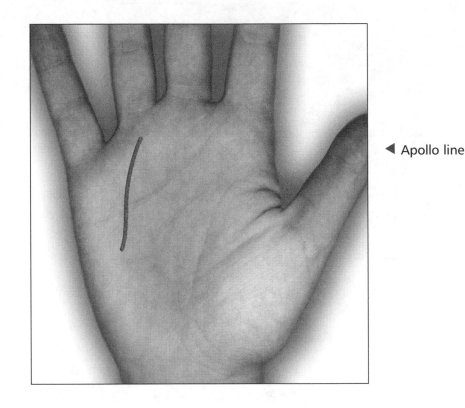

◀ Apollo line

Apollo is not really a planet—it represents the Sun, but it nevertheless belongs in the heavenly band that has a representative in the vertical lines of the palm. The Apollo line generally begins from the Luna mount but may originate elsewhere, and it traverses the palm to the mount of Apollo.

The Apollo line can be irregular or strong, but its presence is a good indicator of the overall success of life. A stronger line signifies reaching a goal; a weaker one shows the problems encountered along the way. If it begins at the fate line, it means that that is where your successes began. Apollo lines are usually an indicator of individual, not group, success.

If the line begins late on the hand, it may mean that success has been delayed until that point. If it is missing entirely, it may mean that you place little importance on worldly success, or it may mean that you do not believe you can achieve your goals and have given up.

Because Apollo is also the god of music and art, the line of Apollo may represent creative ability. However, if there are two or more lines, you may have too many talents to be able to master any of them.

All of the markings that affect the major lines will affect the Apollo line as well:

- Bars can be read as obstacles.
- Islands generally represent periods of frustration and loss of confidence.
- Stars signal important events, especially financial ones.
- Breaks indicate troubled places in an otherwise successful life.

Beyond the major vertical lines of Mercury, Mars, and Apollo, there are others of great importance. You may not have them, but if you do, it tells a great deal about you and how you will live your life. Read on to find out what they are!

The Simian Line

When the head and heart lines are conjoined, the resulting strong line that crisscrosses the palm is known as the simian line (or simian fold). The line is called "simian" because a similar line appears on the palms of many nonhuman primates, particularly apes.

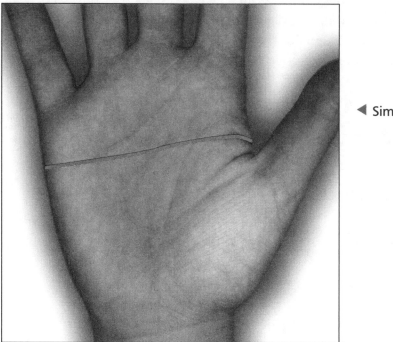

◄ Simian line

If you have a simian line, don't let it make a monkey out of you. It doesn't mean that you are less than human or not bright. What it does mean is that you have a lot of inner struggle and will have a hard time living a tranquil life.

It is best for those with a conjoined head/heart line to make sure that they have balance in their lives between these two forces and that they are very careful in paying attention to the intellectual as well as emotional aspects of life.

Deciding which should take precedence for you, the head or the heart, will be a difficult matter, and you may spend your life trying to find out. Unfortunately, this will be a constant struggle and will demand constant effort.

Too Much Focus on Absolutes

Those with a simian line tend to confuse the rational with the emotional and are unable to separate their respective influences in order to let each one guide the appropriate area of life. They tend to think in absolutes and to be very focused on what interests them to the exclusion of other important factors.

This is not always a bad thing, of course, and neither is having a simian line. This kind of intensity could potentially make you egocentric, ambitious, and driven, but such behavior may help you accomplish huge goals. Unfortunately, such intensity also puts you at risk for disaster.

This intensity is often manifested in the attitude toward religion. People who are fanatical about one idea or dogma often have simian lines. Many of those with a simian line reject the belief system they grew up with to accept another, often radical, faith. This kind of absolute change is often seen in other areas of life as well—in a career or lifestyle change, for instance, where the break with the old and the acceptance of something totally new and foreign is radical and thorough.

E ALERT!

Beware: If you have a simian line, in which the head and heart lines are conjoined, you may be more susceptible than others to some forms of heart disease.

Having a simian line makes it hard to interpret what kinds of problems the markings on the line are revealing. It can also be hard to time the line so as to tell when these problems or influences will occur.

The Adornments of the Hand

You can further build on your knowledge of what the markings of the palm represent by looking at some of its more exotic features, like the bracelets, bows, rings, and so forth. Some people have many such lines and features, making their hands an interesting challenge to interpret; others have very few, presenting a much simpler task. But in either case, these ornaments to the hand, with their evocative and decorative names, add interest to the art of palmistry. Sometimes, reading a palm can sound like a dress-up event because of the images that these names convey.

The Bracelets

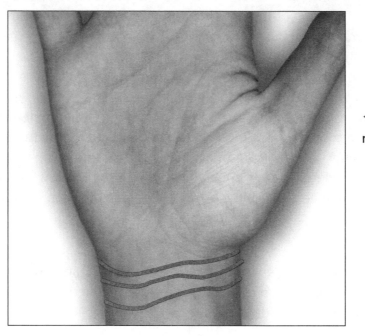

◀ Bracelets or rascettes

The bracelets, also known as rascettes or rascette lines, are a charming attribute that can lead to a greater understanding of what the person will face in life. They are especially highly regarded in the Eastern tradition of palmistry, where the rascettes are a mark of a long life. Every person has some form of a rascette on the hand, and it is located between the palm and the wrist.

In general, the more rings the better, as each ring is said to represent about thirty years in the duration of a life, and a partial ring a fraction of that. It may be hard to get an exact figure, but in general, the longer and stronger the rascette, the longer and healthier the life. However, a chained rascette indicates a life of turmoil.

You should be especially aware of the topmost rascette, the one nearest the palm. If it is curved or broken on a woman's hand, it means health problems specific to females; on a male's hand it signals potential hormonal problems. If you see a star in the middle of the top rascette, look for an inheritance, but if you see a cross, you will have problems as you separate from your family.

The Bow of Intuition

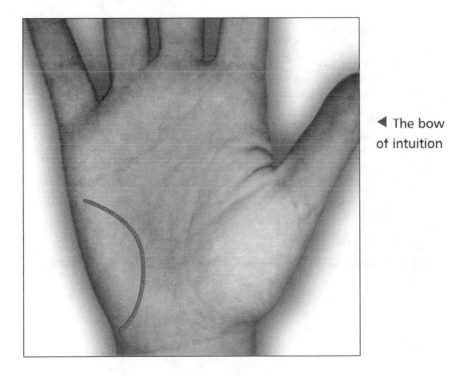

◀ The bow of intuition

One rare palmistry sign is a bow of intuition, a line in the shape of a crescent that runs on the percussion side of the hand from the Luna mount to the mount of Mercury. The bow of intuition is a highly positive sign; the person who has it is likely to be unusually intuitive, sensitive, perceptive, and aware of the thoughts and emotions of others. In other words, the bow of intuition is very apparent on the hands of psychics.

The Fellowship of the "Rings"

In addition to the longer line adornments described so far, the hand may also have rings, or short lines that encircle the base of the fingers of the finger mounts. Each of these rings has its own meaning based on the finger it enhances, and it serves to indicate something of importance about the owner of the hand.

The Ring of Jupiter

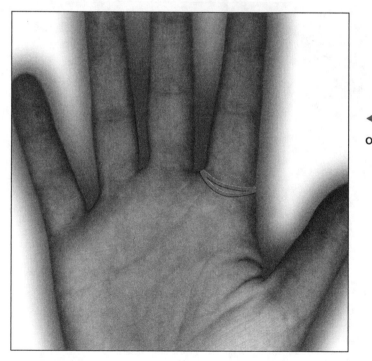

◀ The rings of Jupiter

The ring of Jupiter, found on that mount at the base of the forefinger, is also called the ring of Solomon. Like Jupiter, the leader of Roman gods, and Solomon, the Biblical king, those who have this sign are leaders, persons in authority. At the same time, they are wise and understanding people, no matter what their age. If you have this marking, you are a judicious ruler and a respected and honorable leader.

The Ring of Saturn

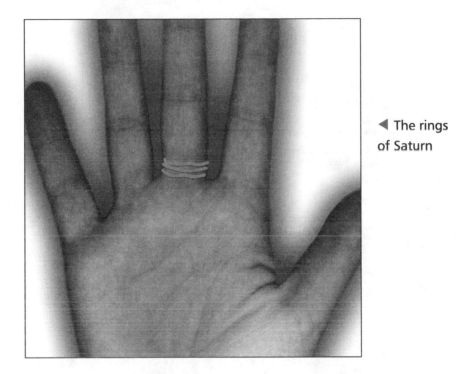

◀ The rings of Saturn

The middle finger, also known as the Saturn finger, may also have a ring, but Saturn rings are not as common. The reading for this ring is very different. While Jupiter signifies leadership, Saturn represents seriousness and dedication, so a ring here shows a serious and unlively nature, and perhaps even a morose one. The deeper and more complete this ring, the more it shows a depressive and ponderous personality.

FACT

If you have a ring of Saturn, take a look at your head line. If it slopes down to the mount of Luna, you have a good imagination. More than likely, it will manifest itself in dramatic tendencies. Who knows? Perhaps you're a natural actor!

If you have a ring of Saturn and your fate line has a negative mark, such as a cross or star, you may ruin your career by not paying enough attention to it. If your ring is made of two lines that cross each other on the Saturn mount, you have a tendency to depression and self-destruction.

The Ring of Apollo

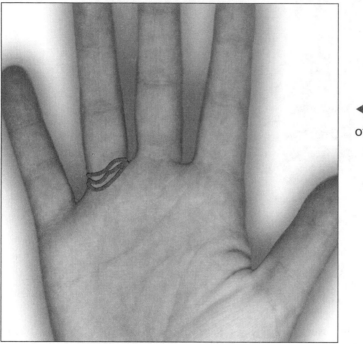

◀ The rings of Apollo

While the other rings tend to highlight the virtues associated with their fingers, the ring of Apollo, a rare mark, acts in just the opposite fashion—it seems to form a barrier to the gifts of Apollo, which are aesthetic expression and a sunny nature. The ring of Apollo indicates a blockage of creativity and potential for sadness or depression.

The Family Ring

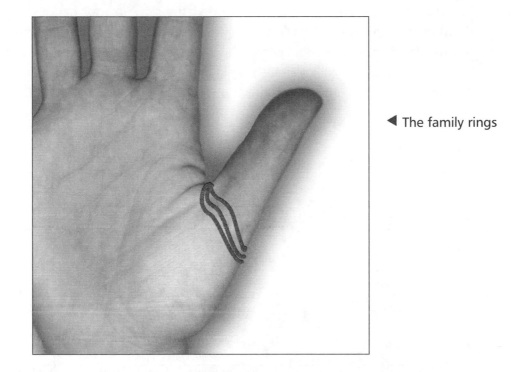

◄ The family rings

A ring around the base of the thumb represents family loyalty. The stronger the line, the more you care about your family, and any interfering lines mean interference from a family member. If there is a second line here, it means a second family, perhaps by a second marriage or by adoption.

Unlike the more easily read three major lines, secondary lines and patterns are often very different from palm to palm. When doing a reading, you should try reading the more dominant hand first, then look at the lesser hand to find out more information about the secondary lines and patterns.

Nine Loops

In addition to the lines previously described, the skin on your hands can hold many other special markings known as loops. Palm loops have the characteristic of looking like lassos. They are not complete circles, but rather open-ended half-circles in various sizes. Not everyone has all of these loops, but if you do, you can gain additional insight into what makes you tick.

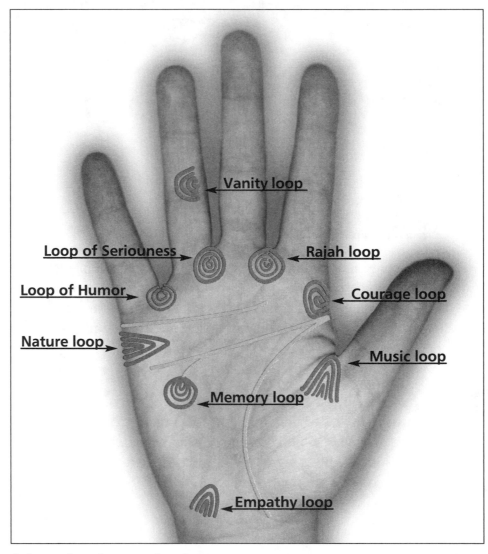

▲ Loops found on your hand

The Rajah Loop

A very unusual but very positive pattern to have is the Rajah loop. You can find it between the Jupiter and Saturn fingers, where it shows your skill at leading, influencing, and motivating others. In fact, it is sometimes known as the loop of charisma.

Look for this loop in those who gather others around them for a cause—religious leaders, activists, politicians, or those who lead their fields in scholarship, business, or the arts. If you have the Rajah loop, make sure that your influence over others is used for the good and not to their detriment.

The Loop of Seriousness

This loop occurs more frequently than the Rajah loop, in one out of five hands, and can be found between the Saturn and Apollo fingers. If your palm displays this marking, you have a mission in life and you are driven to achieve it without wasting any time dawdling along the way. You are a responsible and earnest individual and very motivated toward achieving your end. However, if the loop is more pronounced or noticeable near Saturn, it can point to psychological weakness.

The Loop of Humor

This loop is found between the Apollo and Mercury fingers and indicates a person that likes to have a good time and laugh at life's little ironies. If you have it, you enjoy all the creature comforts and would rather work at something you enjoy even if it does not pay as well as other jobs. In fact, people who have the loop of humor tend to not care much about achieving rank and position.

Oddly enough, you can have both a loop of humor and a loop of seriousness. If both appear on the same hand, it means you take life seriously and respect the drive to achieve your goals, but you can enjoy the path toward that achievement and find pleasure in your journey.

The Music Loop and Bee

This is a rare loop found on people with a strong love for music and an emotional response to it. It is found at the lower end of the hand, beneath the Venus mount. Two such loops, one on each hand, may indicate a career, or at least a devoted hobby, in music.

This is further enhanced by the presence of the Bee, a smaller marking at the center of the Venus mount. It signifies a love not for just music but music played on stringed instruments. Look for this if you play the bass guitar in a rock band or viola in a concert orchestra.

The Nature Loop

This loop is found on the percussion of the hand, either underneath the heart line or near the mount of Luna. Those who possess this loop have a great interest in nature and love to be outdoors or learning about it. They may be good gardeners or veterinarians and seem to have an innate understanding of flora and fauna.

The Memory Loop

About one out of every ten people has this loop and it is found on the outer side of the hand near the percussion. It represents exactly what you might assume it would from its name—the ability to remember things such as facts or events, including their emotive overtones.

If the memory loop is found near the mount of Mars, you have a memory that is good for figures and dates, but if it is in the Luna mount, it can mean you would make a good psychic—very insightful and able to read others accurately.

The Vanity Loop

This rare loop appears on the Apollo finger. This particular loop indicates an overwhelming sense of self-consciousness. If you have this marking on your hand, it could mean that you are far too caught up in how others judge your appearance and you worry too much about your looks. It could also mean that you are too concerned about what others think about you and their criticism. If anyone does find fault with you, you are very sensitive about their comments and take them too much to heart.

The Courage and Empathy Loops

Finally, there are the courage and empathy loops, both of which rarely appear on the palm. The courage loop is a looped marking in the web of the thumb. Its presence indicates a special propensity to bravery and valor, both physical and mental. The empathy loop is found near the wrist rascettes at the bottom of the hand. As you would expect, it means that the bearer is full of concern and kindness, is interested in other people, and is able to establish an empathetic relationship with them.

The Girdle of Venus

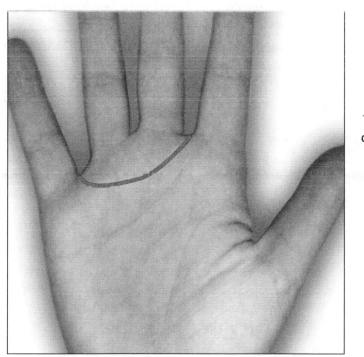

◀ The girdle of Venus

Venus does not have her own finger, but she does have a mount—and a girdle. The girdle of Venus does not appear very often; its shape is a half-circle that runs from the outsides of the Apollo and Saturn mounts. Named after the beautiful goddess of love, both the mount of Venus and the Venus girdle are indicative of your sensibility in love and sensuality, though of course they have many other interpretations in palmistry. This is partly because in the past, sexuality was sometimes seen as a negative attribute. Traditional practitioners often saw an interest in sexual matters as a sign of immoral living and lascivious behavior, or even as an indicator of sexual violence. However, palmists now know that the girdle of Venus is usually seen on fire and water hands, which are more sensitive and vulnerable to emotional reactions to life.

Broken Lines, Broken Hearts

A strong and healthy girdle of Venus correlates to a strong and healthy sensuality and wholesome emotions. It can also indicate a deep aesthetic sense and love for art and beauty, whether it is found in another person or in artwork. Persons with a girdle of Venus can be poets, writers, or artists.

However, a broken line can mean a fragmented sense of love, with too many flirtations and fickleness and too little devotion to the love object. It can also mean too much sensitivity, an inability to control the emotions, depression, or constant upheavals.

If the girdle of Venus crosses the fate line or line of Apollo and overwhelms them in appearance, be warned. There may be a loss of fortune or status, and this may be caused by someone you love.

If the girdle of Venus cuts through a good strong marriage line, there may be hysteria, an inability to balance emotion with any form of reason, and propensity toward addiction to and over-reliance on antidepressants.

More than one girdle of Venus can mean a greater likelihood of a life of vice and depravity. Granted, sensuality is generally seen today as a good thing, but there are limits to everything. This is especially true if the lines are broken or chained.

Markings on the Mount of Luna

Finally, let's examine two kinds of special markings that may appear on the mount of Luna—whorls and composite patterns. Both of these markings usually appear on the fingertips (see Chapter 8) and are very rarely present on the mount of Luna. These are whorl patterns and the via lascivia.

Seeing Whorls

A whorl pattern on the mount of Luna is a sign that you may have psychic or mediumistic skills. Even if you do not, you are imaginative and can envision your thoughts in pictorial images.

If you have a composite pattern where two loops join to form an S pattern, duality is at work, and this duality has to do with your gender identification. In a man, this mark means that he exhibits what are traditionally thought of as female attributes, such as sensitivity, while a woman with this pattern would be direct and aggressive.

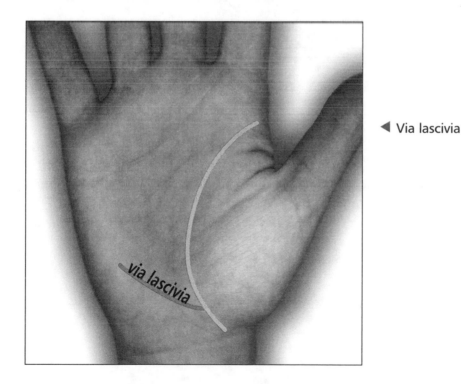

◀ Via lascivia

via lascivia

Via Lascivia

The via lascivia is a horizontal line that crosses the Luna mount. Its name shows that it was originally thought to herald a lascivious nature and that persons with this mark lacked sexual restraint. Now, however, many people say that it indicates a sensitivity to allergies or negative reactions to certain food or chemicals. It is now called the allergy line. Ⓔ

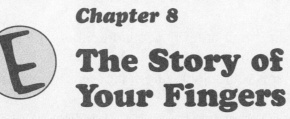

Chapter 8

The Story of Your Fingers

Beyond the palm, fingers have stories of their own to share. Each finger represents a different talent, interest, or ability. If you have a finger that is extraordinarily longer than the rest, that can mean you have one dominant talent or ability. People with long fingers tend to love finer details, while those with shorter ones are more inclined toward manual labor. Let's spend some time doing a general reading of your fingers. Then, the next chapter will continue with what you can learn by looking at fingerprints and fingernails.

Every Finger Has a Name

You may just think of them as your fingers, or tools you use to retrieve things or communicate with others, but in palmistry your fingers are known by their individual, more esoteric names, which correspond with the gods of Roman mythology for their attributes:

- The Jupiter finger is your index finger; it describes your leadership abilities and assertiveness.
- The Saturn finger is your middle finger; it describes moods as well as responsibilities.
- The Apollo finger is your ring finger; it is an indicator of happiness or contentment, and can also show an interest in the arts or sciences.
- The Mercury finger is your fourth or little finger; it shows how creative or emotional you are.

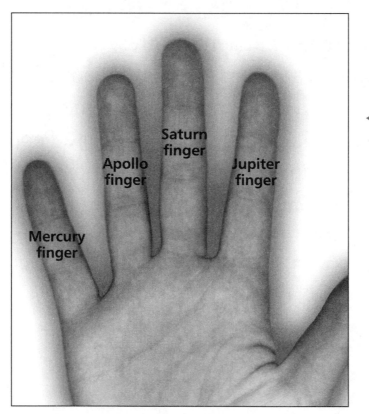

◀ The four fingers

Finger Tips Regarding Jupiter

If the Jupiter finger extends to the base of the nail of the neighboring Saturn finger, you likely have a love of power and a desire to lead others. If it is as long as the Finger of Saturn, though, you can be extremely egotistic and seek to control or overpower others in an unhealthy way. A crooked or bent Jupiter finger shows a tendency to dominate others through unfair means or advantage, while a short Jupiter finger indicates a dislike of personal responsibility.

ALERT!

Fingers set evenly on a line indicate success, but if the Jupiter finger is set low in comparison to the other fingers, your radius of personal influence is hampered and you will not be an effective leader.

Sad, Sad Saturn Finger

The Saturn finger can be a prime indicator of depression. If it is noticeably longer than the others, there is a strong tendency toward depression. A shorter Saturn finger can mean you are generally free from serious depression, but that you are fearful of responsibility and have a tendency to bury your head in the sand when a situation carries the slightest bit of pressure. If your Saturn finger is crooked or bent, you have a real chip on your shoulder—possibly even a persecution complex. As a rule, the finger of Saturn is practically never set low.

Apollo's Fire—and Fame

The finger of Apollo shows your potential for fame. If it's long, you would like to be a celebrity, particularly in the creative arts; if it is excessively long, it indicates a craving for notoriety at any price. If your Apollo finger is short, you shun any kind of notoriety or publicity and prefer to keep a low profile, often working behind the scenes. A low-set Apollo finger means that while you may have an interest in pursuing an artistic career, you may not have been born with the talent to make it happen. See page 130 for more information on finger length.

Mercury's Balancing Power

Your Mercury finger holds the balance or abuse of power. If it's long, you have the shrewd ability to exploit the skills and talents of others for business purposes. If it is extremely long, extending past the base of the nail of Apollo, you can be a bit of a hypocrite. A short Mercury finger means that you have an inability to use your own talents to the fullest, but don't like to capitalize on the talents of others. If your Mercury finger is set low, you are likely the imaginative, dreamy type—both of your feet are up in the clouds, making it difficult for you to earn a sensible living.

Not All Thumbs

The thumb is one of the most important character divulgers on the hand. It shows your degree of self-control and personal willpower, as well as your disposition, and should always be read together with the head line.

The length of your thumb is significant. A long, well-formed thumb indicates a strong will and sound judgment. A short, thick thumb means you can be quite contrary or stubborn—it's your way or the highway, and opposition from others only tends to make you more convinced that you're right.

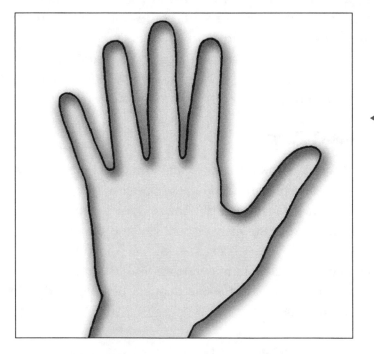

◄ A long thumb

◀ A short thumb

The Right Angles

Let's look at the angle at which your thumb joins your hand, since this has direct bearing on your sense of justice and fairness. When it's close to the palm, at an acute angle, you have a more conservative nature and believe that everything should be viewed in terms of black and white. You just don't like to dive below the surface—your reality can be cut with a fork and knife. You follow the rules, pay your bills, and move on to the next experience.

The more idealistic types have a thumb that forms a right angle with the palm. If this is how your thumb is positioned, you are much more willing to see things from other perspectives, and have a strong sense of justice that leads you to give others the benefit of the doubt. Innocent until proven guilty is your credo—and you will always look for the positive in every problem or situation.

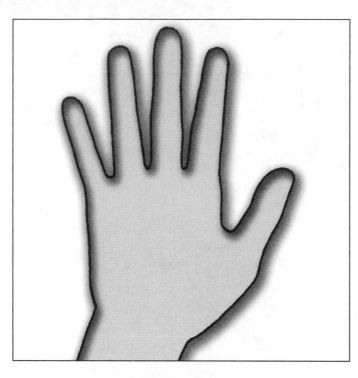

◀ Thumb at an
acute angle

◀ Thumb at a
right angle

Joints of the Thumb

The joints of the thumb are divided into three sections, sometimes called phalanges, and each one relates to a certain ability. The top phalange, or nail, is devoted to personal will or strength. The middle phalange pertains to your ability to reason, and the phalange at the base of your thumb indicates your capacity for love.

ESSENTIAL

In Eastern palmistry, the phalanges of your thumb can also be said to correspond to three aspects of your life: the physical (closest to palm), practical (the middle section of your finger), and mental (the fingertips). In fact, the same divisions may be applied to your fingers.

When the first and second phalanges are of equal length, you've got a great balance between your willpower and sound judgment; however, if the first phalange is much longer, your willpower is weak when weighed against your wants and desires. Consequently, your judgment can be impaired, and you may wind up with exactly the opposite of what you were attempting to achieve. If your first phalange is thick or clubbed-shaped in appearance, you are likely a person who will resort to angry, violent outbursts to achieve what you most want. Anger management therapy is highly recommended for these types!

When the second phalange is much longer than the other two, you are a person who can think clearly and logically enough but you may not have the right amounts of determination and concentration necessary to pull off your dreams. This can make you very unhappy, jealous, or suspicious of the success of others. You are convinced that you are intellectually superior in many ways, so why didn't the same success come your way? More than likely, it's because you have a weaker will, and this can be overcome with harder work; you should realize that what comes naturally to some people can also be yours with a little extra effort.

If you have a firm-jointed thumb, you have an obstinate will and strong determination. You enjoy healthy competition and are unafraid of challenge. You delight in proving your abilities to others: If someone says,

"It can't be done," you consciously set out to prove otherwise. You can be narrow in your views or opinions on life and are quite secretive and cautious in your ability to trust. But despite your competitive nature, you like to play by the rules, and if you do accidentally break a rule or two, you feel tremendous guilt and it really weighs on your conscience.

If yours is a supple-jointed thumb, you are more reasonable and adaptable. You can be easily redirected in your thinking, sometimes too easily to be considered credible. You don't need competition to succeed; all you ever need is to have your curiosity piqued or your imagination sparked. If your boss or coworkers really want you to succeed, they will praise you often and not place you into highly competitive situations. You are generally more tolerant, open, and giving than those with a firm-jointed thumb, and you give your thoughts, time, and cash more freely to those who seem in need. You are more concerned with intention rather than hard-and-fast rules, and will consider lobbying for change when it's for a cause you strongly believe in. You don't mind hearing some criticism along the way, either—especially when you're sure you're helping others.

FACT

One specific type of thumb is not better or worse than any other. Your thumb's shape can give you information about your potential for ambition and talent, but you should remember that you can overcome any limitations you have inherited in this life!

Other Types of Thumb

Also note what the top of your thumb looks like. The "waisted" thumb looks like it has a waist line, formed by the narrow joint that connects the second phalange to the top of your thumb. This type of thumb represents an unwavering tact and the ability to understand lots of different viewpoints. If you have a waisted thumb, you're very empathic and relate well to others. You probably volunteer in a capacity where you are supportive of others. You are enviable in the sense that you have a good balance between your creative and practical sides.

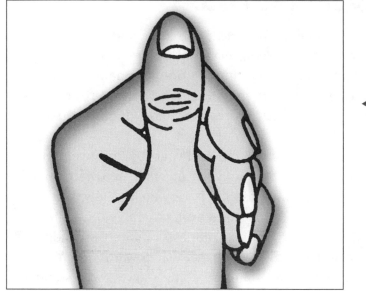

◀ A waisted thumb

If your thumbs are squared off at the top and shaped like a hammer, you are likely to be into excess of one sort or another: perhaps you shop, eat, or drink too much. The challenges associated with this shape can be overcome in life with a healthy balance, so learn to pace yourself!

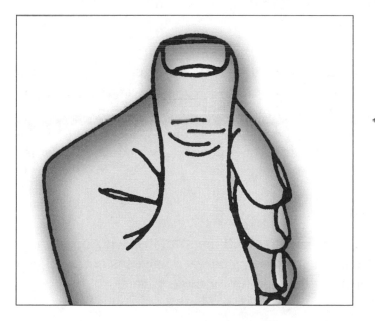

◀ A hammer thumb

Which Way Do They Go?

Now that you've examined your thumb, how about the four fingers? Hold your palm in a normal, relaxed position. Which way do the fingers seem to lean? Is one finger more dominant than the others? Note which one is more dominant and be sure to review this finger's meaning, since it obviously marks your most dominant personality characteristics.

If all of your fingers incline toward your Jupiter finger, you are a highly ambitious person. If all of your fingers lean toward your Saturn finger, you are a person whose life is very melancholy. You have an almost gothic desire to be different from others, and usually set yourself apart from them in negative ways that assure you of solitude. Believe it or not, many comedians have fingers that lean toward a dominant Saturn finger, proving that laughter can overcome sadness with some ambition and hard work.

ALERT!

When you are reading palms for others, they might become very self-conscious at this point. To prevent a person from fidgeting, ask that he or she place the elbows on the table and drop the hand that you aren't reading down until you are ready to switch hands.

If your fingers lean toward your Apollo finger, you are passionate in your pursuit of an artistic or creative profession, and you have your heart set on becoming well known for your talents. If all fingers point toward the Mercury finger, you have incredible business acumen and should pursue entrepreneurial interests, especially if your Jupiter finger is long and slender.

Wide, Open Spaces

Now relax your hand to check the natural spacing between fingers. More often than not, the spacing between fingers is not at all even—there is a dominant space between two or more fingers.

A wide space between the Jupiter and Saturn fingers indicates an independent spirit or a free thinker, while a wide space between the Saturn and Apollo fingers indicates an ability to rise above challenging circumstances. A wide space between the Mercury and Apollo fingers means you act independently, much like an entrepreneur.

Sometimes, all the fingers are straight and equally spaced; if yours are configured in this lucky manner, you will achieve everything you set out to do in life without much struggle or angst. You are blessed!

Finger Shapes and Meanings

Just like the five hand types, the fingers can be shaped in five different manners, each having a separate and distinct meaning in palmistry. The four basic shapes and their corresponding meanings are:

- **Conical:** These are the fingers of wise, old souls who possess terrific insight and inner knowledge, as well as creativity; these are great friends and supportive people.
- **Pointed:** These fingers point to expensive, eclectic tastes and a great eye for style and décor. Those with pointed fingers are also deeply spiritual and intuitive.
- **Spatulate:** These fingers indicate predominance of the intellect; people with spatulate fingers tend to be witty and interesting, with many layers to their personalities. They are also serious workaholics and can be obsessed with success—but they always make time for serious adventure.
- **Squared:** These fingers signal the need for simplicity and are common with people who are direct, fair, and considerate. These folks are quite willing to work hard for what they want in life, making them ideal business people who lead by positive example.

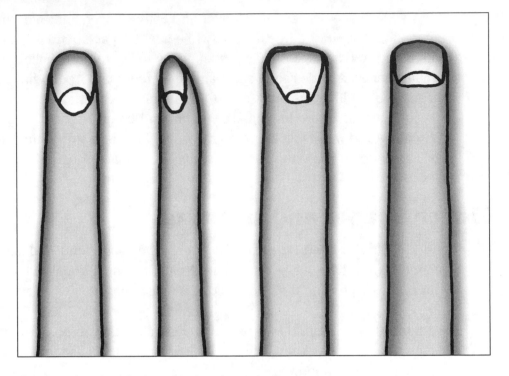

▲ Conical, pointed, spatulate, and square fingers

Mixed finger shapes are very uncommon; a person whose fingers have elements of two or more shapes have a tendency to be unpredictable—they show one side of themselves to the outside world, and have another side that is distinctly different and completely private.

Smooth or Knobby?

Are your fingers looking a little like they've been through the wringer? If you think you have "knobby" fingers characterized by knots in your finger knuckles, more than likely the cause is rheumatism or arthritis—but some knots can occur naturally without pointing to a specific illness.

Knobby fingers without a medical explanation speak to mental capacity, particularly the ability to analyze situations and come to the correct conclusions about them. People with knots in their finger joints sometimes stew over the little things in life, but have a knack for stepping up to the plate when an emergency situation arises.

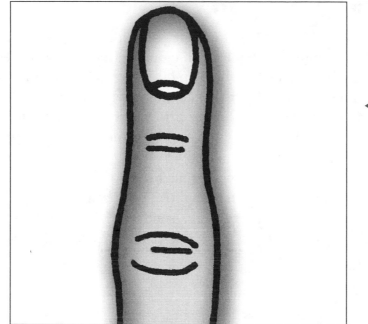

◀ A knobby finger

People with smooth fingers are much more impulsive than their knotted-fingered counterparts. They often mistake their own hunches for proven truth. They don't always think before they act, and end up being surprised that their actions have manifested the situation they most wanted to avoid. Often, they just don't understand how their actions will affect the lives of others, and as a result, others see them as cold or self-absorbed. They can take an unmovable stance on a subject, often flat-out refusing to change their minds, even when the truth becomes known.

You should never try to argue logically with a smooth-fingered person; instead, try persuading them by helping them to experience the truth, make them think the correct conclusion was their decision, or let them make their mistakes and learn from hard experience.

ESSENTIAL

When the knots occur between the first and second joints of the fingers, this means you have an almost-supernatural power to analyze the complex—you can see things that aren't clearly visible to others. The knots separating the second and third finger joints indicate the more mundane ability to analyze people and things.

Finger Length

Now that we've looked at finger shape and joints, let's move on to length and its meaning. The total length of a finger can be measured from the center of the knuckle to the tip of the finger. A finger is considered to be short if it doesn't reach the joint immediately below the nail on the next-longest finger. A finger is long if it exceeds this joint in length and extra long if it is the same size or larger on what is usually the next-longest finger.

As a rule, short-fingered people are interested only in quick results. They can see people or situations with broad perspective. If the hand has a strong thumb, a long first finger, and a solid head line, short fingers can have quite a capacity for work and don't mind "pulling the wagon" or doing their fair share of work.

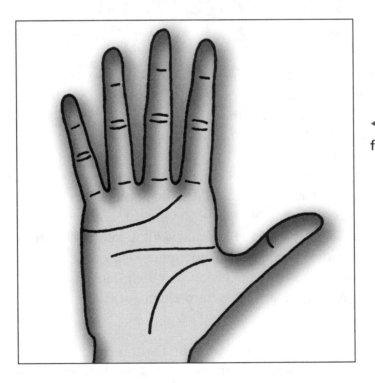

◀ A hand with long fingers

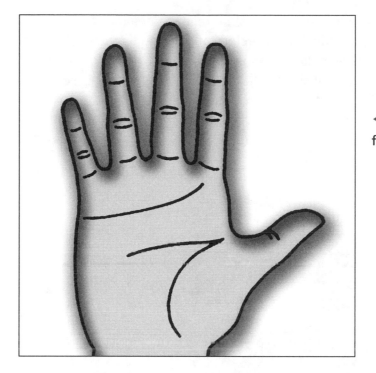

◀ A hand with short fingers

Do you have long fingers on your hands? Long-fingered types absolutely adore details and are good "idea" people. If your fingers are unusually long, similar to the pointed or psychic type of hand, you are likely a person who gets so wrapped up in ideas and possibilities that you never act on them.

Reading Finger Lines

As an even deeper indicator of your obstacles or challenges in life, your fingers can have vertical or horizontal lines on them that correspond directly to the areas of your life represented by each of your fingers.

If you have horizontal lines on your Jupiter finger, it can mean that you will experience a breach of confidence; on your Saturn finger, the same lines reveal worries or insecurities about your home or personal life. Horizontal lines on the Apollo finger depict opposition to your happiness—and those threats may be more apparent in your married life if the horizontal lines are plentiful on both the Saturn and Apollo fingers. On the Mercury finger, horizontal lines can point to sexual inhibition or difficulties.

Vertical lines on fingers pertain directly to health problems. On the Jupiter finger, the thyroid is affected; on Saturn, it's the pineal gland that's the problem. Vertical lines on the Apollo finger relate to the thymus, which can in turn mean that the cardiovascular system is somehow impaired, with blood pressure too high or too low. Have your thyroid gland checked if you have vertical lines on your Mercury or little finger. Vertical lines can also mean you have issues pertaining to poor circulation or high blood pressure.

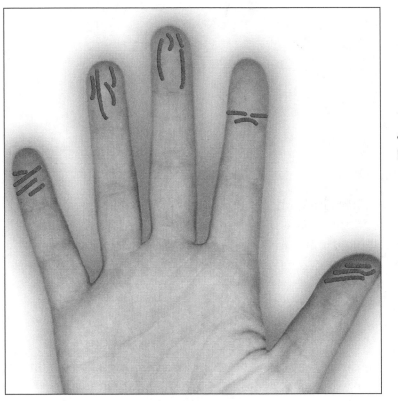

◀ Horizontal and vertical lines

If you have lots of short, horizontal lines on your fingers, you probably suffer from excess stress and should try relaxation or meditation techniques to help calm your nerves. Lots of vertical lines typically mean hormonal problems. For instance, a woman with lots of vertical lines on her fingers might suffer from PMS or hormonal imbalances.

Power over Your Troubles

Most health problems can be overcome with early intervention, so use these lines as warning signs and go to your doctor for regular checkups. It will be interesting to watch your horizontal and vertical finger lines change as you deal positively with each health challenge that presents itself; remember, the lines change as we change.

As a final note, many fingers feature a combination of both horizontal and vertical lines, which means you have the power to overcome the obstacles associated with each finger or aspect of your life. If your fingers contain mixed lines, you are blessed with the ability to come through obstacles smelling like a rose!

Getting a Pulse on Your Future

Before you finish the cursory reading of your fingers, let's do a last-minute vitality check. Does circulation seem healthy in all of your fingers, or are there lots of blotchy spots spread from knuckle to fingertip?

If you see lots of white blotches on otherwise healthy-looking fingers, you likely suffer from circulatory problems and crave physical warmth. If the blood seems to be flowing normally and you have lively pink fingertips, you are healthy and very interested in staying so. Your fingers carry "vital signs" of their own, and they can change from time to time—so check them at least once a year to be sure your circulatory system is spreading its wealth.

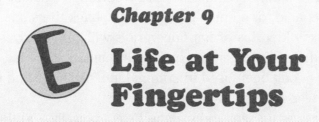

Chapter 9

Life at Your Fingertips

Your fingertips are how you connect to the world, and they let the world connect to you as well. On the front of your hand, you have prints composed of ridges and valleys, and these offer untold possibilities of interpretation, as each one is unique only to you. And when you turn your hands over, your fingernails provide additional clues to your personality and behavioral characteristics, as well as your health.

Uniqueness of Your Fingerprints

Unlike the lines of the palm, the lines on the fingertips, which are your fingerprints, never change. Each print is unique to that person—like snowflakes, no two fingerprints are alike. And no matter how hard people have tried to get rid of their fingerprints—even by burning or cutting the prints away with fire, acid, or a knife—they still grow back the same way. And as the child gets older, his or her fingerprints will grow in size—but the child will keep the same fingerprint pattern throughout life. That is why fingerprints have long been used in criminal investigations and for identifying persons who have been missing.

Fingerprints can now be kept and matched electronically and the Federal Bureau of Investigation (FBI) has more than 70 million prints on file, where they are considered a great asset in crime fighting.

The idea that fingertip skin holds patterned prints was documented way back in 1823 by a Czech doctor, and it was first used for identification in the latter part of the nineteenth century, an innovation that inspired Mark Twain to write a book based on fingerprint identification. The first criminal tried and found guilty on fingerprint evidence was sentenced in 1902.

Patterns and Their Meanings

Fingerprints are found in three basic patterns: loops, whorls, and arches. Each of these patterns can then be broken down further into sub-categories, and each kind of pattern can give you valuable insights about yourself. You may have the same pattern of print on each finger, or they may be mixed. If you have the same pattern on all ten fingers, the attributes signified by that pattern will be strongly displayed.

You can also tell something about what the pattern means by where it is placed. If the center of a pattern is found on the upper part of the fingertip, it represents an intellectual or mental area of concern, but if it is lower, it shows a practical way of dealing with physical matters.

QUESTION?

I have many different kinds of fingerprints patterns. Which one do I use to explore my personality?
Look at all the different types of patterns on your fingertips and determine which one you have the most of. The dominant pattern will tell you more about yourself.

A Pattern of Loops

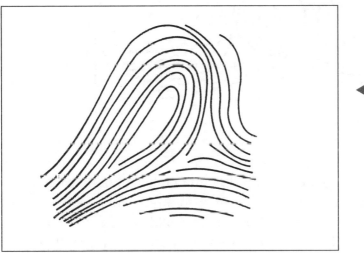

◀ A fingerprint loop

Loops are the most common pattern found on fingertips, especially on the thumb. People with a lot of loops get along well with everyone. If you have them, you are very adaptable to new social situations and interested in everything and everyone. You like to talk to people and find out more about their interests and ideas, and can be a capable or charming leader as well. However, you have to be careful to make sure you assert your personality in social situations. Also, a loop shows that you have very middle-of-the-road ideas in the area represented by the finger that the loop is found on.

There are two kinds of loops: Ulna loops are more common; they come in from the ulnar side of the hand (the outside, small-finger side) and point toward the thumb. Radial loops are more unusual, and they come in from the opposite direction, the thumb. People with these loops are still agreeable and enjoyable, but they are more likely to speak up for their own interests and stand out from the crowd than people with ulna loops.

Whorls Apart

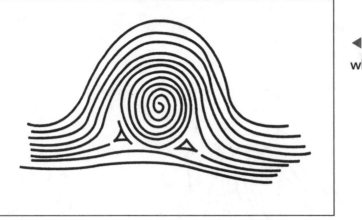

◀ A fingerprint whorl

People with whorls, which look like circles, have a strong will and are more controlling and individualistic than others, but they can also be uniquely dynamic and creative—in a "tortured genius" kind of way. They dislike doing anything the way others would like them to and conforming to a set standard. If you have a lot of whorls, this means that you may have many talents, and you are a decent and trustworthy person.

Whorls come in two varieties—spiral and concentric. Spiral whorls are in the shape of spirals, just as the name suggests. If you have these, you are likely adamant about your beliefs and will hold them faithfully throughout life. You like to be independent at work and you labor best when guided by yourself.

Whorls that form complete and unspiralled circles, which are known as concentric whorls, are unusual and can be usually found on the Apollo or Jupiter fingers or on the thumb. If you have concentric whorls, your attitudes are even stronger—you'd like to be running the world! Fortunately, that wouldn't be all that bad, because you are a responsible person, trustworthy to the extreme.

Strength in Arches

People with arches are hardworking, capable, and commonsensical, and they do not procrastinate when it comes to getting the job done—they can be trusted to follow through. They like knowing what they are getting into, and they are private and down to earth, but they can also have a very limited or narrow viewpoint.

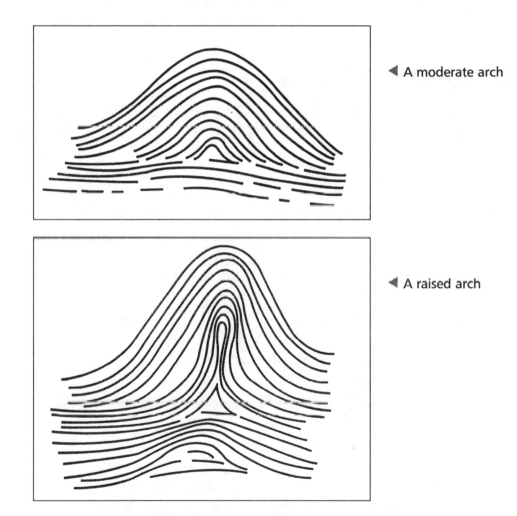

◀ A moderate arch

◀ A raised arch

Don't expect that the fingerprints of your family members will be very similar in pattern. No two people will have fingerprints that are exactly alike—not even identical twins!

Additionally, if your arches are raised, a rare condition with the center part sticking up fairly high around a "tent pole," you are a little more likely to be enthusiastic and idealistic about your life and to let your feelings conquer your practical side. In fact, if the arch is too high, you may be a little too emotionally sensitive, to the point of being nervous and jumpy, unlike the average down-to-earth arched personality. Tented arches are generally found in the fingerprints of emotionally insecure people, while simple arches are typically found in the fingerprints of easygoing folks.

Composite Patterns

Loops, whorls, and arches may also form composite patterns. One such pattern is formed by two adjoined loops, a rare occurrence that indicates either that you are able to see both sides of an issue, or that you are indecisive and cannot come to a conclusion easily. If you have two adjoined loops on your fingertips, you would probably make a good judge, arbitrator, or therapist because you are willing to work for fairness and justice.

◀ A composite loop

The Peacock's Eye

Another form of print where two patterns come together is the Peacock's Eye. This rare pattern, a whorl surrounded by a loop, looks like the eye marking in the tail of a preening peacock. If it is found on the Apollo finger, it protects you and brings luck, but if it is found on the Jupiter finger, it means you have special insights. It can also be found on the Mercury finger, where it is a lucky sign as well.

A Mixed Blessing

If you have a mixed pattern of prints, as most people do, you should look for a predominant pattern that represents the majority of your fingertips and assess yourself in that way. You can also consider each finger separately and judge what influence the pattern on that finger has in that area of your life.

The thumb, for instance, signifies the energy you have to expend toward reaching your life goals; the Jupiter finger, your achievements; the Saturn finger, your stability and safety concerns; the Apollo finger, your hopes and dreams and whether you have attained them; and Mercury, your relations with others and how you communicate with them.

Let's look at what the various patterns mean on each of the fingers:

- **Jupiter finger:** A whorl indicates that you are a unique and unconventional thinker. An arch shows your ability to fix things, whether it is a computer glitch, a clogged sink, a ruined recipe, or a life problem. A raised arch shows dedication to a social cause, combining justice with enthusiasm.
- **Saturn finger:** A whorl indicates that you have an unusual occupation or pastime. An arch means you have good insights about how to invest your money and other strategies for enhancing your financial security. A raised arch means you do these things as well, but with great interest and joy. And a composite pattern on this finger means your indecisiveness extends toward your career path.
- **Apollo finger:** A whorl is the sign of an artist, designer, or otherwise creative person. If you have an arch, however, your abilities as an artisan lie in the crafts—woodworking, metalwork, glass, or maybe ceramics. A composite shows that your taste in art is varied, and you are constantly redecorating or buying new clothes to express yourself as your ideas and opinions change.
- **Mercury finger:** The only pattern of significance on the Mercury finger is the whorl, which demonstrates special talent as a writer or speaker.

Thumb Prints

A pattern on the thumb relates to the way in which you approach life's tasks. A loop, the most common pattern, shows that you are well balanced and sensible. A whorl shows that you are strong-willed and bent on doing things your own way. An arch shows that you take on challenges in a realistic and down-to-earth way, and if it is raised, you do so in a very passionate way. A composite pattern on the end of the thumb shows that you might take a long time to complete a task as you must conduct research beforehand and tend to worry about all the issues involved.

Nailing a Good Reading

Now, it's time to turn your hands around and look at your fingernails. Your nails are vital as protective elements of your body, shielding that marvelous mechanism, your fingertip, with its mass of nerve endings that connect you to the world.

FACT

A healthy fingernail, one that indicates a balanced and successful person, should be a little longer than its width and slightly curved rather than flat, although not so curved it hooks downward at the end.

The fingernails have a lot to tell you—in fact, some signs are very obvious even to the untrained eye. People with a sense of pride will care for their nails, while no grooming and raggedy cuticles on the hand signal carelessness or slovenliness. Bitten-down nails show tension and worry, either as a way of life in a nervous personality or else as a reaction to a temporary problem. Beyond that, the shape, texture, growth patterns, and color of your nails can provide the palm reader with a lot of information about your personality and behavior, and even your health.

Nails of All Shapes and Sizes

The shape of your fingernail is the most important part of interpretation for what it says about you. In order to read the shape of your fingernail, you have to look at the living part of the nail, the part that is the color of your hand, to see what shape your nail is in. (The white part has already stopped growing and is being pushed along by the newly forming nail under the skin.)

Long or Short?

Nail length can be quite a useful barometer of internal pressure and stress. The longer the nails, the more stress or nervous unrest the person is likely to experience. Still, in spite of some nervousness or excitability, long-nailed people can also be amazingly calm, kind, and patient. They are also said to be creative: A long nail shows a good imagination, a sympathetic nature, and an open and accepting personality.

Nail length also indicates the amount of productive energy. Short nailed people typically have more energy, perhaps because those with long nails tire easily from their many intellectual pursuits. A short nail shows an impatient, argumentative, and mistrustful nature. You may be a hardworking and dedicated employee, but you can also be too critical as a boss and too controlling, a micromanager. You are proud and hate to lose any battle, and you may be witty and self-confident, but far too often at another's expense.

Thick nails often belong to people who are frail or sickly, while thin nails belong to the healthy and robust. Wide nails mean you are a plain speaker, a what-you-see-is-what-you-get personality, while narrow nails belong to the more eloquent and polished.

People who have shorter-than-average nails are good critics and love to debate all the hot topics of the day. Although they have quick tempers, they can usually keep it under control, and most people don't think of them as argumentative. If your shortest nail is square at the base, you can take it a step further—you don't just get mad, you get even.

A Geometric Reading

Also, see if your nails can be categorized according to their shape:

- **Square:** A square nail indicates a good temper, broad-mindedness, and a pleasant disposition. If your nail is large, so is your heart—you are agreeable, warm, and trusting. But the smaller the nail, the more mistrustful and cold you will be.
- **Rectangle:** If your thumb has a rectangular, horizontal nail, you are forceful and sometimes quarrelsome and prefer to express yourself quickly and loudly—and then become calm again when the storm subsides. If you have a broad nail, you can be strong and stubborn, but you are optimistic and look to your strength to get you through life.
- **Wedge:** Wedge-shaped nails are narrow at the bottom and wide toward the top. These nails belong to nervous people or those who have been under a lot of stress. Maybe it grows in this form to make it easier for you to chew on. At any rate, find a way to relax more.
- **Oval:** An oval nail is the kind seen in hand lotion commercials, and it generally represents a gentle and sweet soul with a strong emotional life. However, you may be too gentle and meek, and should work on building physical and mental stamina.

If your nail shape dents in when looked at from a sidewise view, look for a nutritional problem or iron deficiency. And a nail that goes in the opposite direction, downward over the tip of the finger, can indicate a respiratory problem.

Fingernails may also have marks that offer further indications of personality and challenges. For instance, you might have specks that indicate health challenges—or perhaps horizontal or vertical lines, indicating worries that are more practical in nature.

Growth Patterns

You should also look at the growth pattern of the nail to get insights about your health. Vertical ridges that run the length of the nail show a tendency toward having joint, digestive, or dermatological problems. Horizontal ridges that run across the nail signify nutritional problems. However, if you have only one horizontal ridge or groove, it means you have undergone a great trauma or illness.

Gazing at the Moon

At the bottom of the fingernail lies the moon—that white, rounded part at the cuticle line that is most easily seen on the thumb. Your fingernail is being produced below this cuticle line, and the moon is actually part of the root of the nail, so the condition of the moon is a good indicator of your health.

If you cannot see the moon, it may be a sign of bad circulation, low blood pressure, or general poor health. If there is a large moon, there may be high blood pressure, an overactive thyroid, and perhaps an overly sensitive disposition. Ideally, your hands should show good clear half moons, which indicate a good temper and healthy heart.

Color Counts

It is also possible to tell a lot about you by looking at the color of the nail. The color should be lighter than that of the skin of the hand itself and it should be of a consistent hue, pinkish in the hands of people with primarily European ancestors, tan in persons with Asian forebears, and beige in the hands of those of mostly African ancestry.

If your nails are too pale, you may be iron deficient, and if they are too red, see a doctor about your circulatory system. Spots and blemishes can indicate a vitamin or mineral deficiency. A reddish nail can also mean that you are too hostile and impatient, while a white or gray hue can be a sign that you are self-involved and not enough aware of others and their needs.

Your fingertips, then, offer a wealth of information about you, and as you reach out to grasp your life, you should let that information guide you in ways that will enable you to make that life a fuller and healthier one.

FACT

You might see little white spots on your nails. If they are not the result of an injury, these may have been caused by a nervous strain. In fact, these spots are sometimes called worry spots.

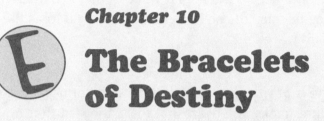

Chapter 10

The Bracelets of Destiny

In a complete palm reading, it's important not to overlook anything. One part of the hand we haven't covered yet is the wrist and bracelets (the wrist lines known as the rascette). These lines, which loop around the bottom of the wrist like bracelets, mark the entryway to the hand—the place where the skin patterns begin and the reading of the palm can commence. Traditionally, rascette lines were thought to be an indication of longevity, but there are many other pieces of information that they can tell the palm reader.

The Rascette

Each person in the world has some form of wrist lines on the hand, and they are considered one of the nine sets of minor lines that bring extra interpretive information to a hand. Collectively, the wrist lines are known as the rascette, and there are generally three of them (though in some cases there may be four); these lines may be referred to as the first, second, and third rascette.

The rascette is of vital importance because it connects the hand to the brain that thinks, the heart that feels, the feet that travel, and the chemicals in the body that create the lines of the hands.

When you are examining the rascette, don't read further than where your wrist bones meet the radius bone on your arm. When reading rascettes, you always want to stay focused on the major lines around the wrist.

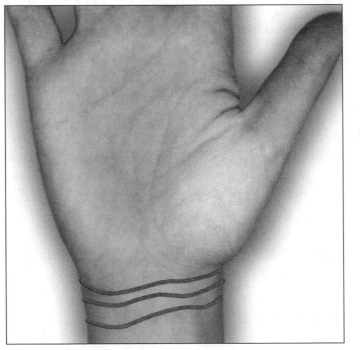

◀ Bracelets or rascettes

Traditional Ways of Reading Wrist Lines

In Eastern countries, where hand reading is more respected than it is in the West, the wrist lines and other minor lines are thought to be far more important than they are in Western palm-reading traditions, perhaps because they resemble the graphic symbolism of the written Asian languages.

The lines of the wrist are especially highly regarded in the Eastern tradition of palmistry as an indication of longevity, and they are used to determine whether the owner of the hand will have a long life. Indeed, some practitioners call them the bracelets of life. According to some of the methods of interpretation, each of the lines of the wrist is thought to represent about thirty years of life, and the possession of a part of a wrist line would give an additional number of years in proportion to its length. That is, a rascette with three complete and clear lines represents a substantially long life.

Other Approaches

Other systems, dating far back into the past, allot only twenty or so years to a completed and clear wrist line and read the quality of each fraction of life in the clarity and length of a particular wrist line, starting with the first. Thus, the first rascette (the one closest to the palm) indicates the quality of the first two decades of life, the second the next two, and so on. Still others say that the length of lines indicates the length of life, so a line that stretches across the entire wrist means a lifespan of about twenty-five years of good life.

ESSENTIAL

Also found near the rascette at the bottom of the hand is the empathy loop, which means that the owner is unusually able to bond with others and has a great deal of sympathy and concern for others

As a general rule, though, you can read the rascette lines by knowing that the larger the number of lines, and the stronger those lines are, the longer and healthier your life will be. It is also wise to remember that longevity and the expected life span were a quite bit shorter when the maxims and lore of palmistry were being developed. A lifespan of sixty years was astounding then, but today we expect to live a far longer and healthier life.

The First Wrist Line

The first wrist line is perhaps the most important of the rascette, as it is the closest to the palm and most indicative of what lies therein. A reading of the rascette always begins with the first line.

A clear and deep line here shows that the owner of the hand is in good health and physically fit. If your first line is poorly formed and unclear, it means that you are indulgent and reckless, and that your problems may be more of your own making than you would like to think. In general, as with all the wrist lines, the clearer and stronger the line, the better the physical condition of the owner of the hand.

This line can also represent specific health problems. If the first wrist line curves upward into the bottom of the palm or is broken up to a large extent, it can mean gynecological troubles for females—from barrenness to menstrual problems to difficulty in giving birth. In males, it signals urinary, prostate, hormonal, or reproductive problems.

E
ALERT!

Be careful when you are making any statements about someone's health. Clearly, a reading cannot by itself diagnose a health problem. As with all medical indications, of course, look for other indicators before making any judgments.

As always, any look at the length of a person's life must be a balanced one that takes any number of indications into account. It must also be remembered that the lines only show probabilities and that the length and health of a life is largely dependent on an individual's personal decisions.

The Rascette and the Travel Lines

It is wise to remember that the travel lines that often appear on the Luna mount actually begin on the rascette, which is seen by many as a good indicator of a person's wanderings throughout life (see Chapter 17).

However, there is another set of lines that represent important, life-changing trips or journeys. These lines don't go toward the Luna mount but move upward. Generally speaking, the length of the travel line will tell you how long the journey will be and how far you will go. And the straighter the wrist lines, the safer the passage on your journeys through life will be.

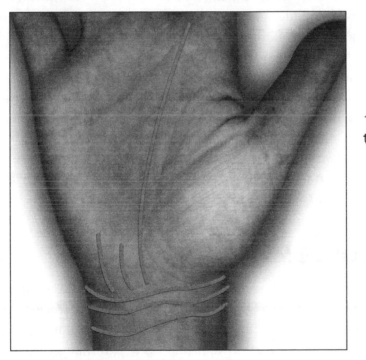

◀ Rascette and travel lines

Moreover, the markings on your life-journey line can tell you about its outcome. If a travel line ends in a cross, the trip will be an unprofitable one; if it ends in a square, the trip will bring danger but deliver you safely from it. A line ending in an island means a loss of some kind, and the bigger the island, the worse the loss.

If the line crosses the palm near the thumb and ends at the Jupiter mount, the trip will be a successful one and you will achieve the purpose you set out for, attaining power and prestige as the result of a long journey. If a similar line goes from the rascette to the Jupiter mount and actually crosses the Luna mount on its way, that trip will be by sea.

More Travel Ahead

Other lines from the rascette have meaning as well with regard to travel. A line that travels upward from the rascette to below the Apollo finger means that the trip will be a success and lead to honor and renown for the traveler in that country, in addition to wealth. And even if "the prophet is without honor in his own country," that trip abroad will lead to fame for the traveler that continues after he returns home.

A journey that is indicated as a line from the rascette to the Mercury mount will result in a fortune granted in an unexpected manner as a result of the trip. However, a line that travels from the rascette to the Saturn mount will be, as is characteristic of that mount of seriousness, a troubled trip full of hazards that may well end in catastrophe or death. Also beware of two travel lines that rise from the rascette and cross near their ends, as this means an unpleasant and troublesome journey from which you may not return.

The Question of Marriage

Other interpreters see the lines that rise from the rascette in another way, as representing a marriage. (Of course, in times past a marriage very often indicated a life-changing journey.) According to this style of interpretation, a branch to the Jupiter mount on your hand is a sign that you will marry into wealth and power. A branch to Saturn would mean marriage to an older person. A line that extends from the rascette to the Apollo mount represents a marriage to a person with creative talents and artistic tastes. Finally, a line to the Mercury mount means, as you might expect, a union with a businessperson or merchant, or a marriage as a result of commercial activity, for instance, to someone you met on a business trip.

The rascette marks the beginning of your fate line (or line of destiny), an extremely important area, and the closer this line is to the base of your wrist, the sooner you will learn to be independent and directed. As with the other major and minor lines of your hands, be sure to read both wrists for the best assessment of whether you're meeting your life's true potential.

Reading the Wrist Line Patterns

The lines of the wrist can have all of the markings—crosses, chains, breaks, stars, and so on—that are seen on the other lines, but on the rascette they may have their own particular meanings specific to their location.

- A chain around the wrist can symbolize a life of struggle and hard labor. However, one positive note is that this work will eventually result in a monetary reward.
- A star on the first line of the wrist in the midsection of the line means that the owner will inherit money early on.
- A cross on a wrist line means that the owner will have trouble early in his maturity as he sets out on his own. His family of origin may intrude on his independence and keep him from making that break into adulthood.
- A break in any one of the rascette lines shows a person who is untrustworthy and self-centered. The uncontrolled behavior exhibited by this person will ultimately lead to his or her own downfall.
- If the rascette is crossed by an angle, the owner of the hand will be rewarded near the end of life by financial or career advancement.
- A triangle is also a good sign, as it brings good luck, financial gain, honor, and prestige.

Though the rascette lines are considered minor lines and overlooked by many as unimportant, they have much to tell us about health, travel and marriage, and they are one of the easiest areas of the hand to read clearly. Ⓔ

Chapter 11

E

Reading the Lines of Time

The three major lines, as well as the fate line, can be broken down into time increments that denote or predict specific types of events in your life. These time lines can be used to monitor not only what is in store for you, but also when you may expect it to occur. Each mark or deviation on the lines of the palm indicates some event or situation in life, and timing the lines makes it possible to foresee what possibilities may occur.

Growth and Development

Let's start at the beginning. When a baby is born, his or her hand will show three major lines—the life line, head line, and heart line. Shortly thereafter, other major and secondary lines such as the fate, Apollo, and Mercury lines will begin to emerge. Does this mean that the baby is predestined to live a certain kind of life, based on the lines seen on those little hands?

Not at all. It is vital to remember that the shapes of the lines on your hands will change as you develop your own unique personality and make your own choices about the world you discover. Just as your body is a reflection of the life you live, so are the lines on your hands. The direction you will take in life will shape not only your life—it will shape the lines in your hands, too.

As children mature and become not only more aware of the world but also more in control of their lives, their hands will begin to showcase what they are becoming. That is why hand lines can help you assess a person's characteristics and attitudes, and look out to see what the future is likely to hold for them.

ALERT!

This chapter will give you the tools you can use to estimate the timing of certain life events, but remember that timings on the lines of the hand are always approximate. You can't ever predict a specific time and date of any event just by looking at the palm!

Lines Created by Life Itself

The body has a way of taking in life events and making them a part of itself. We are basically shaping our own destinies through our conscious or unconscious decisions, and our emotions and thoughts come into play. They in turn affect the brain and the chemicals in the bloodstream, which then work to put their stamp on the body—and on the lines of the hands.

Much of this work is hidden from us, and the effects caused by our current thoughts and emotions may not take place or come to fruition until we are much further down our own life road. Therefore, the lines in our palms become the heralds of where our present course of action is taking us and can serve as a guide to let us know the consequences of our present action and what to do to create the best possible future for ourselves. What the lines indicate is not the future set in stone—they indicate possibilities, the general direction to where you are headed.

Because of the physiology of the body, the lines on the palm will come to reflect the passages of time, so you are able to get a glimpse of how life has developed and how it may develop in the future. The major lines of the palm can be subdivided into time segments that will allow you to know the approximate time of what you will be experiencing in that area of your life.

Planning for the Future

When you know what events and situations are coming in a certain part of your life, you will be better able to prepare for them, be they good or bad. And if you know how long any period of upheaval will last, you can gather the resources needed to deal with any problems or shortages.

For instance, if career problems loom, you can exercise care with money and avoid major purchases; if your health might be in jeopardy, you can be sure to seek timely medical advice and also live in the healthiest and safest possible way to avoid illness and accident.

Getting a Clear Time Line

Determining the timing of the life events seen on the palm is somewhat imprecise, as hands will be of different sizes and shapes. However, no matter what the size and shape of the hand, the line you are reading will show a succession of situations and an ordering of events that will be of extreme importance in your overall interpretation. You must learn to time the line you are studying—that is, to look at the line as a whole and see where the events on it fall in relation to your life as a whole. To do this, you will draw or envision imaginary lines (or real ones, to practice) that represent the sweep of years going by.

Imaginary Time Lines

It is up to you to determine what time increments to use, but many practitioners have found that it is easier to use a decade as a measure and divide the lines according to the single digits, teens, twenties, thirties, and so on (then, you can make more detailed observations within each segment). Each increment should be about a quarter inch in length.

Timing life events should begin with the life line. To be able to determine when an event will take place, construct an imaginary gradation line that curves around the life line. The beginning of the life line, above your thumb, represents the time of your birth; the end of your life is where the line ends, around the wrist area.

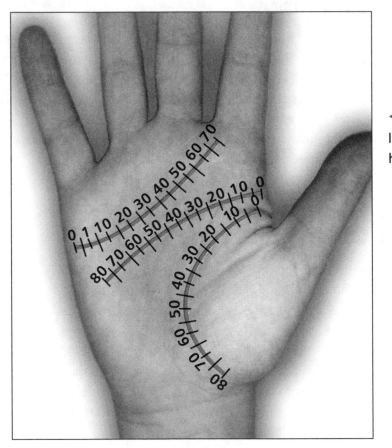

◀ Timing your life, heart, and head line

You can take an impression of the hand with fingerprint ink or even a good photocopy and work from it to learn timing. However, it is best to make minimal use of such methods, as you do not want to obscure any important markings visible on the hand itself.

Next, take a look at your head line, which begins in the same general area as the life line and moves across the palm toward the percussion, and your heart line, which is above the head line but runs in the opposite direction, starting at the Mercury mount. In your mind, imagine both of these lines with time line gradations, going from zero to eighty.

Following Chronology

When you are interpreting, you will find that the marks on the lines give an indication of what took or will take place chronologically during that time. The space on the heart line show events that have to do with your emotional and interpersonal life. The head line will relate recorded events detailing your intellectual development, mental health, psychological viewpoint, and even intuition. Events on the life line show the unrolling of your physical growth, the state of your health, and even your motivation and reaction to life events.

If the life line has a long overlap, be very accurate in determining the point at which the second section starts. The line from the time web will carry over to the new section on a horizontal, representing the age at which a major change will take place in the person's life.

Matching Time Lines to Events

In this way, by drawing these web lines that cross the major lines, you can time the events that take place on the lines. You can now go on to interpret events on the heart, head, and life lines for any time period. You might begin your reading at the beginning of the person's life and work your way around to the end, or else concentrate on a particular time period of interest to the person whose palm you are reading.

Of course, you need not actually create a physical web in order to pinpoint the events on the lines so accurately, though it may be helpful to do so when you are learning. It is often enough just to estimate, moving from the top of the hand to the bottom, just when an event will take place or a situation will develop in your life. This will get easier the more you practice your craft. You might want to start by using a drawn web with some understanding friends to get some experience in timing and then move on from there as you gain expertise. Using different people will also help you understand different sizes and shapes of hands.

Reading Your Fate

The fate or Saturn line shows the broad picture of how you will go through life, so it is important to know where along the time line of your life the intersections, branchings, breaks, and other markings can be found. The time line for the fate line is a little more difficult than for the other lines, as it is more individualistic, but applying the principles outlined here will give you a good start.

First, find the beginning of your fate line, at the bottom of your palm by the wrist, and move upward to the mount of Saturn, breaking it up into imaginary increments. Envision or make a mark halfway along this line to represent the middle of life at about age forty. From here, envision or mark the decades in somewhat even increments, with the beginning of life represented this time at the bottom of the hand and the end at the top.

However, because the events we experience earlier in life have more weight in determining who we are and what we become, the lower portion of the time line may be accentuated and given more space, while the upper part is foreshortened. Overall, most people have found that young adulthood, the years between adolescence and midlife, leads to the greatest variety of events as we develop our adult personas and create a place for ourselves in the world.

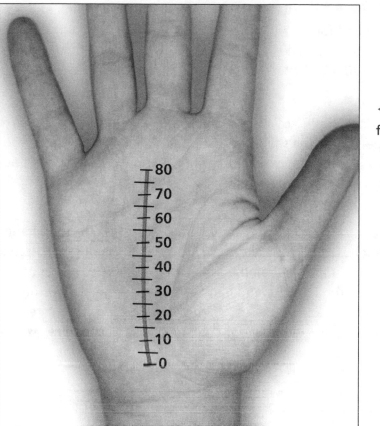

◀ Timing your
fate line

It may be helpful, at least until you have learned to envision the
time segments on the lines successfully, to draw them in onto the
hand with a pencil or a very fine-tip pen that has washable ink.

Typical Time Lines of Life Events

Now that you understand how the timing of the various lines is
determined, you can begin to interpret them. Think of the lines of your
hand like rivers that take you on your life's journey. This journey can be
short or long, placid or rough, successful or a failure. You can learn to

read a line just as a riverboat captain reads his river, looking for shoals and snags and rapids, where extra attention must be paid. A time line serves the same function as a riverboat chart, pinpointing areas where you need additional attention to get through them safely.

ALERT!

Check the timing of events or situations by looking at what is happening at the same time on other lines. This will help you to better interpret what is going on in any particular area, as all life events will have an effect on each other.

Branches from the lines are one place to begin. Like tributaries on a river, branches can shoot out from the lines, and being able to time the line will let you know when this will occur. Branches are especially important on the fate line and can be read by seeing which finger they veer off to. For example, a branch that flows out from the fate line all the way toward a particular finger mount indicates a successful event relating to that finger. Following are some general meanings of these lines:

- A line to the Jupiter mount means that you will accept a new role of importance at that point in life.
- A line to the Saturn mount indicates new responsibilities will be taken on or financial gains will be made.
- A line to the Apollo mount refers to a personal victory that will be achieved at that time in life.
- A line to the Mercury mount represents financial success or that a creative activity will be undertaken.
- An unbroken line from the fate line to the Luna mount shows a successful relationship.

FACT

A line that goes toward a mount but does not successfully reach it can mean failure in that area, or at least incomplete success. To find out what effect the relationship has on the life overall, look at the fate line beyond the branch from the Luna mount for an indication of how it influenced life at that point.

Trouble Ahead?

There are many other signs you may see in a palm reading that indicate problems or challenges along a line that you are timing. Here are some of them:

- **Trauma line:** If a short bar cuts across a line, it represents a temporary obstacle to be overcome, an emotional upheaval like a problem at work or home. Timing will let you know when such obstacles should be looked out for.
- **Islands:** Each island represents a major change in your life; unlike a trauma line, it has an element of duration to it. It represents a situation that is frustrating and longer lasting, such as joblessness or illness. Use timing so you can anticipate and prepare for these situations.
- **Breaks:** An interrupted line that continues later on shows that some change, like a new job or relationship, will take place. If the break is a clean one, the change was not voluntary, and therefore more traumatic, but if the two ends overlap or continue parallel for a while, the change was a planned, purposeful one.
- **Stars:** A star created by several bars on a line shows a very surprising and major change at that point in life, enough to overwhelm the individual whose hand is being studied. Again, being prepared by knowing when this will happen will help you overcome the problem or lessen its effects.

Rarely can a specific catastrophic event be predicted in the lines of the hand. When you are doing a reading, try to focus on general possibilities for life events rather than worrying about making specific predictions.

Once you've practiced a little, signs like these will become as clear as they are to a navigator reading a river map. And, as with a river map, a successful navigator of the palm lines can get a good idea of when you'll arrive at a particular changing or stopping place in life. Learning to time the major and minor lines of the palm is a vital part of palmistry.

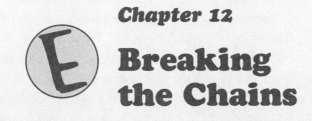

Chapter 12

Breaking the Chains

Up until this point, you may have seen signs of negative life events clearly appear on your palm, and you must remember that these lines only point to potential—and you are always free to make different choices about all the things that happen to you in this life. If your palm is warning you of a traumatic experience that is to come, it's your responsibility to make the changes in your life that will prevent the trauma from occurring.

Major Life Changes

Your life changes as each new stage of it unfolds—and nowhere is sudden or major life change more apparent than on the palm of your hand. Most commonly, change is recorded on your hands in the form of specific markings such as breaks; islands; crosses; or weak, indifferent lines.

Breaks in any major (or even minor) lines almost always represent a change of path—a disruption or redirection of energy. They can be either negative or positive, depending on the lines immediately following and the direction in which they point. A break that points inward (toward the thumb) means a new enterprise or business interest; a break pointing upward (toward the fingers) represents spiritual epiphany; a break pointing outward (toward the percussion) means a sudden adventure in your life; a break pointing downward (toward the wrist) means a total change in lifestyle may be in the works.

ESSENTIAL

If you have a strong, deep life line, you can likely cope with nearly every challenge life may bring. Conversely, a weak or broken life line can point to low vitality, or coping skills that require the help of another person.

But what about other major life changes that can be depicted on the palms of your hands? How—and where—do they show up? Almost always, big changes (such as divorce, illness, career change, or spousal loss) show up on the fate line.

- Divorce is most commonly represented by a major break in the heart line.
- Major illness turns up on the life line as a weak segment to the entire line—if you see this mark, check the time line of the hand to see when you may expect the illness to set in (see Chapter 11).
- A big career change is typically noted by a break on the head line followed by a branch that veers off the broken line in a downward position.
- Spousal loss can be signaled on the hand by a cross over the heart

line in the area past the Saturn finger and moving toward the Mercury finger. Such loss can also be denoted by a severe break in the fate line about midway through.

- Loss of a child can be seen as a faint line on the side of the hand, just above the head line on the mount of Mercury.

- Money loss is most easily identified on the hand by the thumb that is curved outward, because it typically represents a person who is generous to a fault, and who succumbs to nearly every hard-luck story she hears. Whether they recognize it through palmistry or not, charlatans can literally spot these generous types from a mile away.

- A major move is indicated as a secondary line after a break on the fate or life line. The longer this broken line, the farther away from your current home you are likely to move.

- A faint or extremely crooked head line can mean mental difficulties that range in seriousness from mild depression or anxiety to full-blown mental illness. The severity depends on the depth and location (i.e., starting point and finishing point, as laid out on the hand) of the line. If the head line begins at the bottom of the Saturn finger, depression will likely follow the person through life. However, keep in mind that depression can be treated by a qualified physician—just because the lines say depression is possible doesn't mean the person has to suffer from it. Remember, you hold the keys to your own future!

ALERT!

If you feel blocked by traumatic circumstances in your life, use the power of palmistry to unlock talents you didn't know you had—then move yourself into action so that you can create new opportunities for yourself.

Marked by Disease or Injury

People often ask professional palm readers how they can read the hands of those who have been in accidents, or who have physical problems with their hands (such as arthritis, carpal tunnel syndrome, or severe dermatitis).

Physical conditions, whether caused by a genetic defect or an accident, always represent a blockage of energy in a person's life. The true extent of this blockage really depends on the area of life affected on the palm. For instance, if a person suffers from carpal tunnel syndrome, a nerve in their wrist area is blocked. The rascettes, or wrist bracelets, represent desires and change. You can infer from the positioning of the blockage in this area that the person in question does not enjoy change and would prefer a sedentary life.

Arthritis and joint-related problems mean you have a tendency to hold yourself back from opportunities in life—and you would do well to seek treatment, if for no other reason than to keep your options open.

FACT

On a female's hand, gynecological problems such as endometriosis and ovarian cysts are often seen in an upwardly curved wrist bracelet in the rascette closest to the palm. Men with hormonal imbalances also have this marking.

If there is a scar on at least one of the hands, the blockage corresponds directly to the area where the scar marks the spot, so to speak. In one case, you might have a scar from a car accident on the Jupiter finger—which means that a prime leadership opportunity has been removed from the person's life path. A scar on any of the major lines marks a change in thought pattern that is well beyond skin deep.

Accidents That Can Change Hands

Often, an accident may mangle a person's hand. If you work with heavy machinery, you run the danger of losing a finger (missing fingers can be a birth defect as well). Lost or missing fingers represent lost opportunities. If you lost a Jupiter finger, you have also lost power or position in life. Those who are missing a Saturn finger may be devoid of feeling. No Apollo finger often corresponds to the inability to communicate effectively. A lost Mercury finger may mean a meek, quiet personality—a situation where flight is always chosen over fight as a response to stress.

What about a missing thumb? Since the thumb represents physical strength and general temperament, a missing thumb can mean a frail physical nature and a meek temperament.

Happy Accidents

While accidents tend to disrupt a life pattern, they are not always for the negative. Sometimes an accident can literally jar a person into action, causing change in appearance, thoughts, and feelings. This can be for the better—a seemingly negative experience can change people for the better.

QUESTION?

Can your hands show exactly how much energy you're putting out in every area of your life?
Your hands, and the lines on them, can show you which areas you're too focused in and which would benefit from more attention. You can literally see your potential—and hope for a better future—just by taking a good, long look at your hands!

The Trauma Drama

We all go through a lifetime of pleasure, pain, joy, and discomfort. Sometimes the circumstances of our births (for instance, whether or not our parents wanted to have a child or whether there were physical difficulties before or at birth) are etched into the palms of our hands as a kind of indelible "permanent record" of initial trauma upon entering this world.

Unhappy Childhoods

Where the life and heart lines begin (and, in most cases, initially meet) in the crease between the Jupiter finger and the thumb, you will often see the scars of rough childhood: vertical lines indicate illness in childhood, while psychological unrest in the early development stages is typically played out in a series of chains where the two lines meet.

The more vertical lines present in the area of early childhood as denoted on the palm, the more severe the illness or physical problem was likely to have been. For instance, a person who was afflicted with polio as a child might well have several deeper vertical lines crossing both the life and heart lines where they initially meet on the palm.

If you see chains linked across the life and heart lines, an unhappy or challenging childhood is likely the cause. Chains are often present in adults who were abused as children, though having these chains is not proof positive that such is the case with you. Worry lines in this same location indicate a childhood fraught with insecurity, brought on most likely by a fretful mother, father, or caregiver.

A Record of Your Adolescence

Just a mere knuckle's length away from the area of the hand belonging to the childhood period is the adolescent period, where the excesses of youth are marked by circles, raised or puffy spots, or even crosses. If there was trouble involving others, there will be clusters of markings scattered around the section of the hand that points to the teen years.

You can almost always see when the person matured and started making better, healthier decisions—or, on the flip side, determine whether they indeed have outgrown their more outrageous behaviors of their adolescent past.

Solving the Problems

If a person is negatively influenced by her family, that may set a trend for a lifetime of obstacles and pain. However, that is not necessarily the case—even in the worst instances, each person has the power to break the chains and live his or her life with joy and contentment.

In karmic palmistry, it is believed that you are born with a destiny that is mapped out in the lines on your hand. But even those who believe in karma agree that you can change your destiny through free will.

In fact, it may work the opposite way—the secret to solving the problem that you are dealing with in your life may be inscribed on your palms. In most cases, the lines of the hands that point to a problem also signal the potential to overcome or triumph over it.

Trauma Lines Represent Troubles

In addition to marks of childhood and adolescent problems long past, you may find other signs of heavy emotional burden and upheaval. Trauma lines are bars that dissect or cut through the life line, or another major line. The longer the line, the more pronounced or severe the problem in your life. As a rule of palmistry, trauma lines stay with you as long as you carry their burdens—or until you have learned the lesson you were obviously intended to learn from the experience.

Be careful not to confuse lines of trauma with worry lines. Trauma lines are thin, vertical lines that cut through the life line (or a major line), while worry lines don't overlap with any other line. Worry lines are signs of inner turmoil.

Signs of trauma may also be conveyed by islands that cut through the life line—they indicate a time when your vitality or zest for living is low and you are in poor health. Islands are not necessarily bad omens, but can represent a period of being extremely susceptible to illness—or, worse yet, being accident-prone.

Lines of trauma can also appear on the other major lines—as well as on the mounts of the fingers and the mounts of the palm. If you want to know what kind of trauma you might be headed for, or which area of your life might be affected by the trauma, write down each area where you see lines of trauma and then look up its correspondence to a specific area of your life. For instance, if you have trauma lines that dissect your life line but also run through your mount of Venus, you may have a challenging, often turbulent love life.

It's All about Choices

What if your family tree is chock full of alcoholics, obsessive-compulsive individuals, or even the occasional lunatic? Are you doomed to a life of genetically predisposed circumstances or characteristics?

While certain lines on your hand can be inherited, you are always the master (or mistress) of your own fate. Palm reading for trauma indicators is not meant to bring you down or to make you worry about things you might not think you have control over; rather, you can use it as a warning signal that you might have a difficult choice ahead.

Lines can change as you change. In fact, they change all the time—from year to year, your lines are not always the same. Studies over long periods of time have shown that many minor (and even some major) lines can be changed by positive intentions and redirected thought. Weak fate lines can be enhanced over time, becoming stronger than even you thought possible. Attitude is everything—it all depends on you.

Exercises for a Healthier Palm—and Future

Besides consciously leading a healthier life based on a positive attitude and better choices, you can also do some things to make your palms healthier—and, in the meantime, change your future a little more for the positive. Over time, new lines can develop—and new lines hold new hope for the future.

Regular hand massage has been known to enhance circulation, and any release of blocked energy in the hands can yield positive outcome in the condition of the skin itself. If skin tone, color, and texture can be enhanced by improved circulation, this is the perfect metaphor for what could be happening in your life if you choose it into being.

Palmistry can be used with psychology to literally provide a "before" and "after" look at the lines on your hand—photocopies can document how different choices in fact created different lines (and a new destiny).

Your hands—and, presumably your future—can also be changed for the better by using skin creams and moisturizers. Cracked, dry skin is sometimes also known as dermatitis—it makes sense, then, that cracked skin can lead to broken lines, which lead to dramatic change (and not always for the better). Buy high-quality skin care products to help keep your skin (and life) in shape—the softer and smoother your skin, the smoother your life will also be.

Finally, for physical challenges such as carpal tunnel syndrome, you can improve the flow of energy through the blocked nerve by exercising with a squeeze ball at least three times per day. This is easy to accomplish, even in the workplace, since the squeeze balls are small enough to be easily transportable in a purse, lunch box, or briefcase. Anything you can do to improve the flow of previously blocked energy will help open your life to new possibilities. Care for your hands and you will also be caring for your own life, opening up new choices and better ways of being as a result.

QUESTION?

Can I try to change the marks on my hands?
You can certainly affect the lines by creating positive change in your lifestyle or attitude, but you cannot physically force your lines to change unless you have surgery. Change your mind, not your lines.

Positive Changes for a Positive Future

As with any new regimen aimed at improving your general health and well-being, know that however small a change it might seem, taking positive steps and preventive measures can go a long way toward a healthier, happier life—free from the binding chains of unhappiness and misery. Remember, your life is up to you—do what you love, and the lines will follow! E

Chapter 13

Finding the Perfect Love Match

Looking for the perfect mate? Let palmistry be your guide, and you will need to look no further than the lines, mounts, and marking on your hands—and the ones on the hands of your potential partner. You can keep your fingers crossed while you tempt fate, but you can't escape the destiny of true love. Don't miss the signs that say, "All systems go!"

First Impressions

What is the first thing you do when you are introduced to a person? In many cases, you shake hands with each other. Thus, the first impression you form about the new acquaintance is made, at least in part, by the type of handshake you receive—its warmth, firmness, and length.

The famous Victorian palmist Comte de Saint-Germain once said, "Never marry a woman with a square hand or she'll rule your life." Of course, for some men, a strong woman is exactly what they need!

Since hands are generally out in the open and are easy to see, you can get an impression about the person you are meeting by simply looking at his or her hand. The shape of the hand can show you the level of passion and feeling in a person, his or her ability to commit, and other important personality traits. It is also possible to see what compatibility there will be between two people by looking at their hands.

Lovers often begin by holding hands, and much can be learned from the warmth of that hand, its stiffness or pliability, and its softness or hardness. Hands are just basically sensual, the organs by which we feel, the way in which we reach out to others, and we can learn a lot about sensuality from them.

The Shape of Things to Come

Remember the four hand shapes introduced in Chapter 2? Well, you can tell a lot just by noting which hand shape your new acquaintance has. Here is a rundown of the interpretations of what hands say about a person. At most, you will get a good idea about the person whose hand you are holding, and at the very least you can meet a lot of new people by offering to hold hands with them.

- **Conical hands:** These are "air" hands; they signal a person who enjoys having lots of friends but who is very choosy when looking for a partner. This person adheres to a moral code and likes routines.
- **Pointed hands:** These are "water" hands; they represent people who bring their naiveté into relationships, sometimes being taken advantage of by those who are not as idealistic as they are. Those with water hands are highly romantic, sensitive to beauty, fond of gifts, attracted to sensuality, and bored by the routine.
- **Spatulate hands:** These are "fire" hands; they usually belong to people who have widespread emotional ups and downs—frequently, their close and caring friends are called upon to support them in crisis after crisis as they change partners. They like variety, excitement, and new experiences in all areas of life, including the bedroom, and they are very physical people.
- **Square hands:** These are "earth" hands. They point to honesty, sincerity, dependability, and support. While those with earth hands may not be the demonstrative types, you can always count on them. Their hands are crafty and have the kind of creativity needed to make a home.

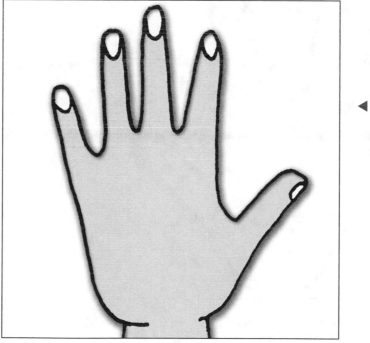

◀ Conical (air) hand

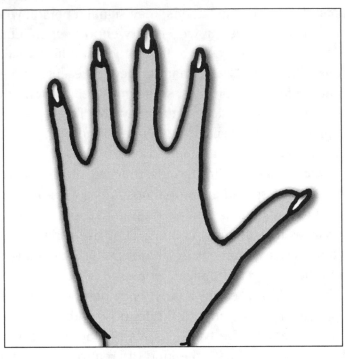

◀ Pointed (water)
hand

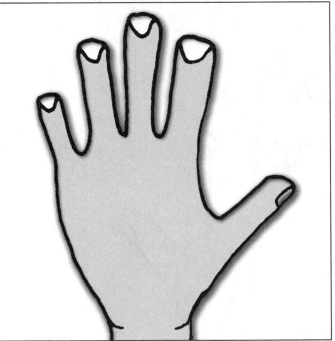

◀ Spatulate (fire)
hand

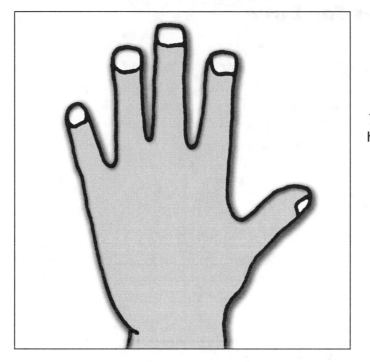

◄ Square (earth) hand

Looking deeply into your individual potential for marital happiness, if you have a well-padded hand, you tend to be warm, passionate, and energetic. You are emotionally healthy and enjoy earthly pleasures, including food and drink. If you have a thinner hand, you are less passionate about life, cooler and more withdrawn. Harder hands belong to those who are less flexible and more demanding of others, while softer hands reveal a lower libido and a passive nature that waits to be given to rather than reaching out to give.

FACT

Relationships can be seen in many areas of the hand: the influence lines, lines of attachment, and lines emerging from the life line, whereas sensuality is seen in the heart line and mount of Venus.

Major Lines for Love

Once you've looked at the basic shape and feel of the hand, it is time to move on to the lines on the palm. Since love and relationships are such a vital part of life, many of them come into play when you are looking for answers in this area. It is the overall pattern of the lines rather than each specific line that will give you the information you are looking for. For clues, look specifically at the heart, life, and fate lines, as well as the markings around them.

The Heart Line

The heart line is a good place to start when looking at your palm to see what your relationships will be like. This line describes both feelings and libido, and shows how well a person manages to bond emotionally with others. If your heart line is long, deep, and without blemishes, you are a devoted friend, secure in relationships, and have an affectionate and loyal nature.

Here are the features that you should look for when reading the heart line for love potential:

- **Chains and islands:** Your feelings are changeable and short-lived. You want intimacy but fear commitment, so you waver and are insecure. Other people may see you as cold and unapproachable.
- **Shape of the line:** If you have a straight heart line, you are very cool and rational, attuned to the mental image of what you want and willing to wait for it. Generally, you are the type of person who makes decisions based on what makes sense. If you have a curved heart line, you are more emotional, moved by your thoughts and desires, and willing to move more physically and aggressively toward goals.
- **Space between head and heart line:** If the space is wide, you are tolerant and willing to live and let live. If the space is narrow, you are secretive and ill at ease in many social situations because you find it hard to say how you feel.

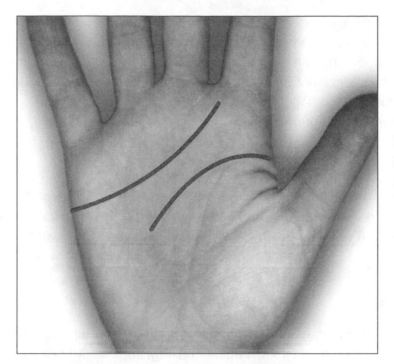

◄ Wide space between the head and heart line

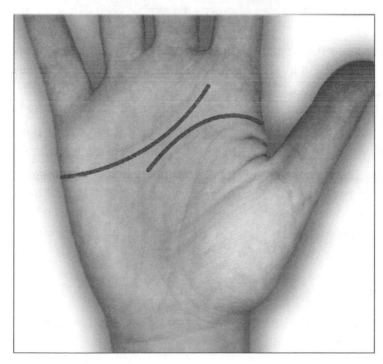

◄ Narrow space between the head and heart line

Also check where your heart line ends. If it tapers off under Saturn, you are a very physical person but one who is controlled by the rationality of Saturn rather than by sheer romance. If your heart line ends under Jupiter, your love life will have a strong component of an idealized view of your partner. You are loyal, but this may veer over into possessiveness. (If your have a curved heart line that ends here, it shows that your love affair may be with all of humanity rather than one person.)

ESSENTIAL

If your heart line ends between Jupiter and Saturn, you can balance between the forces of your head and your heart. You are warm and loving but also can be logical and practical about your partner.

The Head Line

The head line may not be as important an area in terms of providing direct information about your romantic relationships as the heart line, but it will give you valuable clues about your love life as it fits into your overall life.

First, compare the head and heart lines. If the head line is heavier than the heart line, you will look for a partner who can be a good companion and who gives you mental stimulation. You will think before you act on sexual feelings. If the heart line is heavier than the head line, it is just the opposite. You will be ruled more by feelings and your need for passion.

If your head line is straight across the palm, you are practical and realistic about love and you have a less romantic view of things. You also tend to be more traditional about the social mores. If your head line drops downward to the mount of Luna, you are more romantic about love, and the bigger the dip downward, the more imagination and illusion play a role in your hopes and dreams.

The Life Line

Because it lies so near to the mount of Venus, the life line can provide many hints about a person's love life. The life line represents health, so a strong one shows your passion, while a weak one points to a limitation in the amount of energy you have to give to your physical nature.

If you have a life line that makes a wide sweep across the palm, leaving room for a large mount of Venus, you have a great deal of love to give and energy to put to use in the sexual arena. You are likely an extrovert and outwardly directed. On the other hand, a life line close to the thumb constricts the mount of Venus and shows a lower sex drive.

E ALERT! A line that runs parallel to the life line shows that you have a very close and deep relationship with another person who thinks and acts similarly to you. It's likely that this is your spouse, though that's not necessarily the case.

Branches that shoot off from the inside of the life line toward the mount of Venus portray important relationships, either with lovers, close friends, or children; check the time on the life line to see when these relationships may develop. If they continue to follow the line, the relationship will remain strong; if they diverge and head to the thumb, things will get difficult.

The Family Ring

A line circling the base of the thumb inside the life line is called the family ring. It can represent the financial success of the family as well as a marriage. Breaks in the ring of course show divorce or estrangement.

Lines that emerge from the family ring and travel over the life line represent traumas that deal with your family life and that interfere with your romantic relationships. These are more common early in life, while you are establishing your independence and starting your family.

The Fate Line and Influence Lines

While the lines that emerge from the life line are valuable indicators of relationships, you can get the best clues from the behavior of influence lines around the fate line. As you may remember, lines of influence are smaller lines that run parallel or cross over other lines (in this case, the fate line). Those influence lines that emerge from the Luna mount and go toward the fate line are the ones that will tell you something about personal relationships. (For a review of influence lines, refer back to Chapter 7.)

FACT

Influence lines that do not make it all the way to the fate line represent unsuccessful relationships. Lines that meet with the fate line or that run parallel to it are read as successful relationships, and they may be timed by seeing when they arrive at the fate line. You can look beyond the convergence of these two lines to see the effect the relationship will have on your life.

You should also look at how the fate line and the life line are related. A fate line that touches the life line or even begins inside it shows a strong influence of your parents in your selection of a mate. You will want a partner that will help replace the parent of the opposite sex: a fatherlike caretaker if you are a woman and a nurturing caregiver if you are a man.

On the contrary, if the fate line begins far from the life line in the middle of the palm, you will be far more independent in selecting your mate. And if it begins at the mount of Luna, your relationship will be one in which you look for a Godlike and demanding figure to worship.

Lines of Attachment

Next, look for the lines of attachment, which are the small lines beneath the Mercury finger at the edge of your hand. Formerly, these were called marriage lines. Today, we are less likely to think of them that way, preferring to see such important and life-changing relationships in the influence lines.

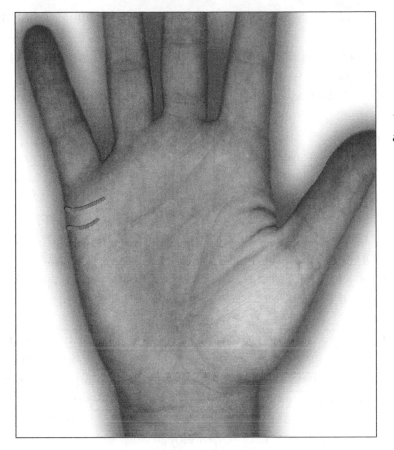

◀ Lines of attachment

Still, the lines of attachment may be seen as indicative of relationships in general—love affairs, very strong friendships, or relationships with mentors or other significant persons. Of all the lines of the hand, they are the most changeable, so it is unwise to read too much into them, especially in regard with divorce or dissolution. Unlike the other lines of the hand, they cannot be timed accurately, so they may be read incorrectly or confused with others.

You can get some idea of when the relationship will occur by noting that the lower they are, the earlier in life you will experience them. The middle point of the area between the base of the Mercury finger and your heart line will be at about age twenty-five, and the point between it and your headline will be at about age thirty-five to forty.

Here is what else you can learn by looking at the lines of attachment:

- If these lines are long, deep, and strong, so will the relationship. It is especially good if the line continues to the Jupiter mount.
- If the lines have breaks or islands, the relationship will suffer breakups, estrangements, arguments, and troubled periods. A bar at the end of the line signifies a sudden end to the relationship.
- A downward turn means a bad end to the relationship; an upward turn, a happy and successful one. (A line with a downward turn used to be called the widow's line as it signified the end of a marriage in a time when death was the usual way for a marriage to end.)
- If a line bends down to touch the heart line, there will be a sudden and surprising end to the relationship.
- If there is a fork at the end of the line, it means the partners will drift apart, even if the relationship will not formally end.

Attachment lines often have vertical lines that meet with them. In the past, these vertical lines were regarded as indicating the number of children you would have (deeper lines for boys and shallower line for girls). Today, this interpretation is seen as invalid. However, the presence of these lines on your hand could indicate you have a special relationship with children as a teacher, coach, or beloved aunt or uncle.

The Venus Mount

Turning away from the lines of the hand, we'll look at one of the most important elements in our sexual and romantic life. The mount of Venus, as you might guess, is where the sexual force lives in the hand—and the higher it is, the sexier you are. It represents not only the generative process but also your capacity to make and keep good friends.

Check the size of the mount of Venus. If it takes up more than a third of your palm, you have a lot of physical passion; if it's smaller than that, you don't really express your passions in a physical way. If the life line goes through your mount of Venus, you do not hold sex as an important element in your life. This is also true if your mount of Venus is flat or small.

One major indicator that you should definitely consider when looking at your partner's hand is the mount of Venus. As it is very indicative of our sexual energies, it is important for both partners to understand its meaning before considering a long-term relationship.

The Girdle of Venus

Find your heart line and look above it for a circular line between the bases of the Jupiter and Mercury fingers. If you have one, it is called the girdle of Venus and is an indicator of a very sexual or emotional nature. (For a more detailed description of the girdle of Venus, refer to Chapter 7.) This is particularly true if it is accompanied by a mount of Venus that is large and strong.

A shorter girdle of Venus is a sign of emotional responsiveness, and it can be found in those in the performing arts who are both sensitive to beauty and who can share it with others. If the line is clear, you can balance your strong emotional responses in a healthy way and not be overwhelmed by them.

On the other hand, a long and unclear girdle of Venus with many breaks shows you will have trouble with finding a good outlet for your emotional responsiveness. You may make unwise decisions or act out in extremely unproductive ways.

ALERT!

If you have a girdle of Venus, beware. This can mean you are looking too hard for a perfect mate who may not exist. Look outside of your imagination at the real world to find your love partner.

A Finger on Your Pulse

Your fingers can tell you something about your relationship interests as well. First, look at the Mercury finger, which reflects the ability to communicate and so can serve as a guide to how good you are at maintaining relationships and discussing your desires and goals. A long Mercury finger is also seen as a sign that you are sensitive to others and sensuous, a good indicator of an enthusiastic sex life. A low-set Mercury finger shows that you regard sex as a primary factor in your life.

A Saturn finger that bends toward the Apollo finger is the sign of someone who needs a great deal of personal space in a relationship. The long Jupiter finger shows dominance and the need to be on top. A short Jupiter finger shows a lack of self-esteem, especially in relationships.

The thumb's angle to the Jupiter finger indicates sexual inhibition. As the angle of the thumb increases, sexual freedom grows. A thumb at a smaller angle to the rest of the hand shows a person who is closed and prudish.

In general, the flexibility of the thumb and hand shows your ability to adapt to others and their needs. This is an important component of a relationship. However, people with very flexible hands may be unpredictable and harder to live with.

Happily Ever After?

If your hand shows that the sexual side of life is not the strongest of your urges, you need not despair. Happiness in relationships is found not so much in the sexual side of things but in compatibility. Good relationships are based on having things in common, and these can be found in many areas: intellectual pursuits, sports, the arts, travel, and the outdoors.

The key is finding a partner with mutual interests and a nature similar to yours. Two people with lower sexual interest will be happier than if someone with a high sexual interest marries someone with a lower interest in the physical aspects of life. Then, too, opposites do attract in certain ways. Someone with a more dominant sexual need might do well to find someone who likes to take a submissive role.

The first place to look for compatibility—be it with a partner, family member, or friend—is in the shape of the hand. It goes without saying that two people with the same hand types will be compatible.

- Two air-handed people can master their emotions and will be on the same mental plane, sharing ideas and activities.
- Two earth-handed people will get along because they work hard to build a solid relationship.
- Two water-handed people will live as soul mates, but their inattention to practical matters may get them into trouble.
- Two fire-handed people may have more of a problem than the other three groups, unless their dips and peaks complement each other's. They must take turns being high and low, seeking and getting attention.

When the hand shapes are mixed, the partners must find ways to overcome their differences:

- An air and earth couple will have to learn to balance their opposing desires for routine and excitement, for seriousness and fun.
- An air and fire couple shares an interest in fun and friends, but air will seek more freedom and fire may be jealous and possessive.
- An air and water couple shares creativity, the water partner can benefit from air's practicality, while air can learn to think on a more visionary level from the water partner.
- An earth and fire couple are both energetic and constructive, but fire may have to become more patient while earth learns to be more fired up about things.
- An earth and water couple is the least likely to get along. Earth is logical and practical, while water is dreamy and aesthetic. They will have to work hard to find a way to coexist.
- A fire and water couple seems like a paradox, but this is a good combination, a passionate pairing if fire takes control and leads water to a more worldly level.

Completing Each Other's Lines

You should compare your life, heart, and head lines with those of your partner to see how compatible you are—and how to make the most of what you have and overcome differences.

When I look at my partner's hands, should I be looking for lines similar to mine?
For life's major areas (career aspirations, money abilities, and interest in children), you'll want some similarities in your lines. But for hobbies, philosophies, and general tendencies, variation is essential in order to keep the relationship alive.

First, look at your heart lines to see how similar they are. If they are the same length and move in the same direction, you understand each other well and have much in common. However, if one of you has a curved heart line, indicative of warmth and spirit, and the other a straight one, showing cooler emotions, this could mean trouble—or a chance to balance each other and work together to create a strong relationship that takes both the rational and emotional into account.

The same is true of the head line. If you have a curved head line and your partner has a straight one, you will differ on issues of practicality and romance. This is an indication that you should bring both of these things into your lives, strengthening your relationship by making it more multifaceted.

Differences in the life line show differing health and energy levels as well as differences between introverts and extroverts, which can be overcome. But if the life lines and mounts of Venus show differences in sexual appetite, these are hard areas in which to find compromises.

Overall, the differences in a relationship must be taken into account. Stresses and arguments that arise from them can cause trouble, or we can use them as ways to learn acceptance and tolerance of differences. At best, these challenges can force us to grow and to learn another person's point of view and expand our own, overcoming our own limitations of thought and behavior. If the devotion is there, it may be worth it.

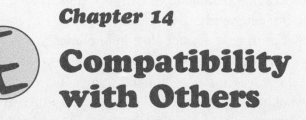

Chapter 14

Compatibility with Others

Hands are the way in which we reach out to each other in love, friendship, and kinship. Since hands are so important to human relationships, it is wise to use hands and what we can learn from them to help us understand our relationships with others, be they friendships, business relationships, or even familial relationships. By looking at the hands of the individual, you can figure out how to build positive connections and what to avoid if you want to establish a nurturing alliance.

Shaking Hands with Destiny

We share much with our friends—hobbies, good times, insights—and often the palm lines of close friends turn out to be very similar. This shouldn't be surprising. After all, if your interests, attitudes, and even personality match your friend's, these similarities can be demonstrated in terms of the similarities on your hands.

If you and your friends are not alike in personality, it is also true that opposites attract, and differing personalities serve to complement each other and bring out new qualities in each other. The hands indicate our strength and weaknesses, dreams and desires, and this is what forms the bonds of friendships. A bold person may help a shy friend learn to come out of herself, while a measured and thoughtful person can check the exuberance and rash behavior of a friend and teach him to think about the consequences of his actions before he acts.

ALERT!

Look at how a potential business partner holds his or her hands. Are the thumbs tucked into a fist? If so, you best avoid placing your trust in this person; such a hand position generally indicates a person who is hiding something.

It's important to know, then, both in personal and in business relationships, what the other person is like, so we can build on commonalities, learn from differences, and find out whether our relationships will work to our advantage or whether they are doomed to failure. Our hands will also help us to see ways to make our relationships better, and will pinpoint areas where we can improve ourselves and learn to understand others so that we can increase compatibility and improve our friendships and partnerships.

Test Your General Compatibility

A place to begin exploring how you may get along with another person in a friendship or business relationship is by looking at the shape and lines of your hands for similarities and differences. Remember that it is not only the similarities that draw persons together but also the differences that complement each other. These allow people to explore new interests and make the most of their own characteristics through the influence of their friends.

Hands of the Earth

Two earth-handed people can make for a good and solid relationship, as both are hard working and practical. They will learn to trust each other quickly and be able to count on each other. An earth-handed person and an air-handed person can be put at odds, as earth faithfully gets on with the task at hand day after day, while the air-handed one seeks new challenges and wants to talk about them before taking action.

Both earth-handed and fire-handed people are willing to put a great deal of time and effort into a relationship. The fires' exuberance needs their partners' down-to-earth practicality to help stay on target, and earth partners need fires' passions to stir them to new enterprises and activities. An earth-handed person mixing with a water handed person can muddy the waters with fighting and incompatibility. Water may find the earth partner seemingly unfeeling and too blunt, but earth does offer a way to bring water's hopes and dreams to fruition with logic and practicality.

Walking on Air

Two air-handed people working together as friends or colleagues will put their brain power to use to achieve rational goals and pursuits, with no side trips into suspicion about other relationships or excessive passion. They should get along well. However, an air-handed person and a fire-handed person love life and socializing with other people—and although this could be fun, the fire-handed person may be too possessive and the air will need to learn to show commitment to the task at hand without feeling overwhelmed by the fire's demands.

An air-handed person with a water-handed person can be a good pairing, but air must learn to live with water's need for complete loyalty and provide emotional support. Air benefits from water's aesthetic sense, and water enjoys air's cosmopolitan nature.

Fire and Water

Two fire-handed people are like two sparks with a single flame—intense and sensitive. They will need to learn to involve each other and be attentive to each other's needs rather than concentrating solely on themselves.

Two water-handed friends or coworkers will become immersed together in their quest for art and beauty, but someone will have to remember to take the bus fare. They will get along just great, but will they be able to survive in the world?

ESSENTIAL

> You can always count on a friend, coworker, or family member whose hands or fingers are square in shape. These people are strong, dependable, and trustworthy.

A fire-handed person and a water-handed person will get along as they are both full of life, emotion, and energy. Fire may have to guide water onto the material and practical plane and away from more ethereal pursuits.

A Linear Relationship

Beyond the hand shapes, friends and partners can test compatibility by looking at the major lines of their palms to find differences and similarities in their characters and the ways they approach life. The three major lines are a good place to start:

- **The life line:** Life lines can show if two people share vitality and energy, important in determining whom to spend time with. A life line with a broad sweep shows a passion for life and others, while a narrower one shows greater inhibition.

- **The head line:** Two people who share a straight head line will also share practicality, and those with curved lines will be more imaginative.
- **The heart line:** Look at the length of the heart line and the direction it takes across the palm to search for compatibilities. Those with straight lines think logically, while those with curved lines react emotionally to stimuli. This is one place where differences can add strength to a relationship, as both responses are needed in life.

Look also at the other aspects of the hand for areas of mutual interest, hobbies, and ideologies. Do you both like to travel? Garden? Are you interested in sports or crafts? And do you have political or religious similarities?

FACT

The St. Andrew's Cross, a small cross between the fate and life lines, is the sign of a person who will save a life (or has already done so). It can also mean one who is giving, nurturing, and brave—good attributes in a friend.

A Mark of a Friend or Business Partner

Finally, you can look at compatibility by looking at specific traits and attributes that you look for in a friend or that make people friendly, and to see what their hands say about them. Characteristics to look for in general relationships should include the following:

- **Friendliness:** A wide life line shows a friendly spirit, and a life line that is far from the thumb shows an outgoing nature, while one close to the thumb shows introversion. An arching thumb that curves backward is the sign of a friendly person, but that friendship may be superficial and may not stand the test of time.
- **Shyness:** If you have a short Mercury finger, you may be part of the 12 to 18 percent of the population who are shy. This is not necessarily a bad trait—many shy people are sensitive and make good

friends. In fact, shyness is a positive asset in cultures that value group identification and are less impressed with assertiveness.

- **Sensitivity:** This trait, which indicates a caring nature, is displayed by the ring of Solomon, which appears beneath the Jupiter finger, as well as by the bow of intuition.
- **Trust and honesty:** A wide angle of the thumb shows a trusting nature, while a narrow angle shows a suspicious mind. A crooked Mercury finger means the person "bends" communications to serve his needs, while a thumb habitually tucked inside the fist shows something to hide.
- **Tact and diplomacy:** All relationships benefit from these traits, which are signaled by the small pads on the insides of the fingertips.
- **Loyalty:** If your head and heart lines are balanced and similar in color and depth, it's likely that you are a loyal friend and business associate.
- **Ability to listen:** Look for a long Mercury finger to find a good and outgoing communicator, one who realizes that communication is a two-way street.
- **Leadership:** A long Jupiter finger is good in a business partner, as the leadership indicated by a long finger means the person is interested in hearing what others have to say.
- **Tolerance:** A wide arch between the thumb and Jupiter finger shows acceptance of others' differences, as can a healthy heart line. A wide area between the heart and head line shows that a person is nonjudgmental.
- **Patience:** If the first joint or phalange of the thumb is shorter than the second, the person is patient; the longer the first thumb joint is than the second, the greater the temper.
- **Sense of humor:** Humor can be seen on the upper part of the percussion with a slight bulge. But if you have a naughty streak to your comic side, look for a wide arch between the thumb and Jupiter finger.
- **Independence or need for freedom:** "Give me my space," says your friend when he feels you are crowding him. A wide gap between the Apollo and Mercury fingers shows that the person may be stifled by too close a relationship.

If your friend or family member's head and life lines are separated, that person is likely referred to as "glue"—this is the person who mixes well with all types of people, and who often brings (and keeps) others together.

All in the Family

Some of the most important bonds you make with other people are familial bonds. While your compatibility with friends and partners is of great importance to you, it is perhaps most vital of all for you to achieve good and compatible relationships with your family members. After all, they are one element in your life that you cannot change.

Luckily, it's almost guaranteed that you share at least some of the hand elements with those of your family members. Although the lines of the hands can and do change in response to life events and our reactions to them, our fingerprints, major lines, and skin ridges show the strong influence of our forebears. And because most people choose their mates from their own group and with characteristics similar to their own, many traits are passed on from generation to generation. Indeed, we can trace family relationships through the lines and shapes of our hands.

A Sometimes-Tangled Web

A family is a complicated web of relationships, with all kinds of alliances and resemblances, favored children, and prodigal sons. The similarities between our hands show the ways we are like our various relatives, and the differences show the variety that exists within a family. Indeed, similarities can create tension and disharmony, as two members of a family may be too much alike to get along, whereas differences between family members can strengthen a family as each can make a unique contribution.

In all cases, it's important in family relationships to respect what the palms and hands tell us about how to deal with the members of our family. This is the best way to build compatible relationships and to make sure our personalities and attributes can be made to work together for mutual growth and happiness.

The Question of Progeny

Children are a big part of the family. Traditionally, palm readers established how many children a woman would have according to the number of small vertical lines that met with the marriage lines beneath her Mercury finger. Deep straight lines were thought to represent boys and shallow or curved lines signaled girls. Today, the interpretation of these lines has expanded—though they may represent your own children, they could also indicate relationships you will have with other children as a family member, teacher, coach, or scout leader. According to one recent approach, look for girls in lines that rise from the attachment line away from Apollo and boys in lines that travel toward Apollo.

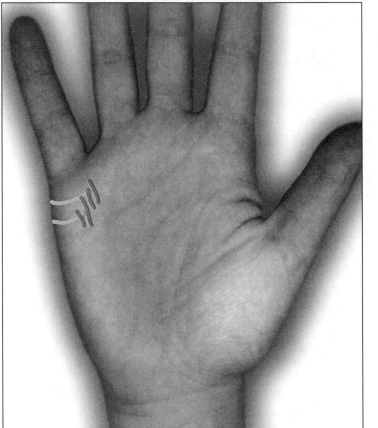

◄ Child lines

E
ALERT!

Pay close attention when attempting to read the children lines; since they are so close in proximity and appearance to stress lines they are often misread. Use a magnifying glass for closer scrutiny.

Another indication of children in your immediate family can be seen in lines of influence that travel from the Luna mount to the fate line. It is these lines that signify successful relationships, including the birth of children and other truly significant events in your life. Look at the fate line beyond its confluence with the lines of influence to see what the outcome of that relationship will be in your life.

Child Rearing

You can learn a lot from reading your child's hands. Use that information to bring your parental attention to particular elements in order to create a healthy relationship with your child. Following are some examples of child-rearing strategies based on the child's hand shape:

- Square-handed children are obedient and respond well to discipline. They may not have an imaginative reaction to life, but you can overcome that by being clear about the practicality of the skills you want them to have. You can also stress a love for aesthetics that augments their own commonsense approach to life.
- Spatulate-handed children need an outlet for their energy; good ideas include the sciences, crafts, and books on travel and invention. These children can benefit from having a routine, but make sure not to do it in a way that will challenge but not alienate.
- Pointed-handed children are sensitive and need sympathy and encouragement to become more assertive and brave. Keep these children active and happy by serving as a role model to overcome negativity and dreaminess, and try to establish a sense of self-reliance, good work habits, and organization so that they can find a place for themselves in the real world.
- Conical-handed children should be given a routine to follow and encouraged to pursue outdoor activities that keep them grounded.

Also encourage practical activities and an independent nature. However, make sure that you fulfill their love for communication via music and books by making these a treat for sustained effort.

If your child has a head line that is close to the life line, encourage him with great praise when he uses his initiative and finds ways to overcome dilemmas. If it is further from the life line, be more careful with your praise, and make sure that he is really trying to do his best and isn't just getting by. Curb his impulsiveness and make sure he learns organization and precision.

Psychic or conical-shaped hands are becoming more and more prevalent on children; metaphysicians believe this is because more children have heightened awareness as a result of being "old souls." In other words, they've lived at least one lifetime prior to their current one.

Children with a thumb at a right angle to the Jupiter finger will have a good sense of fairness toward others and can be trusted in most cases. If the angle is smaller, the child will have to learn to be fair through both lectures and example. And a child with a very large angle to the Jupiter finger may need to be taught not to let others take advantage of him. A child with a curving thumb needs to learn to be thrifty, but one who has a rigid thumb must learn to share.

These are just a few examples of how your knowledge of palmistry will help you become a better parent. There are many other instances whereby you can look at what is written in the lines of your child's hand and find ways to augment the positive forces and introduce skills that will counteract the more negative ones.

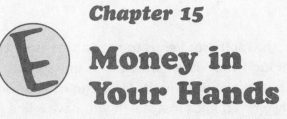

Chapter 15

Money in Your Hands

For some people, money seems to grow on trees—for others, money slips through their fingers, and disappears the minute they get their hands on it. But prosperity is more than the amount of money you have stashed away. It's also in how you make your money—your success in a career or a business. Luckily, you can get a glimpse into the future of your prosperity by looking at the palms of your hands.

The Shape of Prosperity

The shape of your hands, along with the lines on it, can tell you a lot about how you regard money—both how you make it and how you deal with it after you get it. The primary indicator of your relationship with money can be seen in the shape of your hand.

ESSENTIAL

A line rising from the mount of Venus to the Saturn mount shows wealth gained through your own hard work. A line rising from the mount of Venus to the mount of Jupiter is a sign of financial success, especially when it ends in a star. If you have a line from the mount of Venus to the Apollo mount, look for a lottery win or other cash explosion.

- **Air-handed:** These people are savvy about money and how to get it. They have a taste for commerce and a good business sense, are in the know about stocks and bonds, and take care to make the most of their investments.
- **Earth-handed:** These people are careful with money and like to save it methodically in order to be ready for any emergencies. The money that they make is generally earned through hard work.
- **Fire-handed:** These people generally do have enough money, but may be short of cash at various times. Their money comes from a surprising variety of places and in differing amounts, too often through speculation and other risky ventures.
- **Water-handed:** These people rarely think about money and prefer to spend time on creative pursuits rather than entering the commercial arena. Luckily for those who have talent, they will find that their artistic powers may bring them unlooked-for wealth regardless.

The Right Job for You

In addition to finding clues as to how you earn and retain your money, your hand shape can help you figure out what type of a job or career is right for you.

- **Earth-handed:** These people are skilled with their hands and like to work outdoors at a slow but steady pace. They are practical and like to see the outcome of their work and know what to expect each day, so they like to stay with one job. Farmers, loggers, and mechanics are generally earth-handed.
- **Air-handed:** These people like jobs where they have the opportunity to communicate, either in traditional roles such as teaching, law, writing, and politics, or in electronic communications and computer work. They are good administrators and are well organized, and they respect rules and are very reliable. They like to look at connections and relationships, so this group includes engineers and accountants as well.
- **Fire-handed:** These are leaders who like to be in control, and who do well under stress and when challenged. The fire-handed are extroverted, and they like adventure and innovation, so they also excel in the performing arts or safety forces. Business executives and entrepreneurs are also found in this category.
- **Water-handed:** Creative, with innate taste and talent, these people may become sculptors, graphic designers, models, or hairdressers. Because they are usually thoughtful, sensitive to others, and studious, they may also use their talents in the healthcare professions such as nursing, therapy, or library work.

A Part of Your Life

After looking at the shape of your hand, turn your attention to your palm lines for more information about how you get and spend money, your power over it, and its power over you. First off, there are two major lines that must be examined to interpret how you deal with finances: your life line and fate (or career) line.

The life line offers financial and career information. This line is the result of your motivation and strength and shows the extent of your physical and psychological strength to work toward your financial and other goals in a determined way.

> When it comes to your life line and fate line, breaks and branches are indicative of events and situations of importance. Islands are times of frustration, bars represent obstacles, and so on.

If your life and head lines begin together, you tend to be careful and self-effacing, and the longer the two lines run together, the more cautious and introverted you are. On the other hand, separate life and head lines mean that you are a self-confident and impulsive person, and the farther apart the two lines, the bolder and more restless you will be in the work environment.

Examine Your Career Line

Next, take a look at your fate line, which is also known as the career line, along with the Apollo line, which follows it and which deals with overall career success and retirement. The fate line depicts the course of your career and financial life, notes your achievements and losses, and records job changes. It provides a time line to follow so that you can chart your professional and material progress, and it shows financial joys and woes, business setbacks and victories, and so on.

Career Satisfaction

Because the fate line shows your overall career satisfaction and how you've fulfilled your life's work, it becomes deeper and stronger the more you feel satisfied with your career. A weak fate line shows that you have not fulfilled your ambitions; a wavy line means you have wavered in your dedication and spread your energies too thin.

If you have no fate line at all, but the rest of your hand is a powerful and positive one, it may mean that you live a life of adventure and nonconformity. You may have had many different jobs, but your overall life is one of substance, if not stability. However, if the line is missing from a hand characterized by broken lines and with little of a positive nature to note, the adventure and nonconformity shown by the lacking fate line may indicate a life of crime and dissipation.

Signs of Indecision

The presence of two fate lines can mean you have two careers, or perhaps one career and one strong cause or pastime that is like a career to you. Having many weak lines in this area means that you have not yet determined your life work and are instead pursuing a wide variety of unfulfilling jobs.

> A line rising from the mount of Venus to the Saturn mount shows wealth gained through your own hard work. A line rising from the mount of Venus to the mount of Jupiter is a sign of financial success and especially when it ends in a star. If you have a line from the mount of Venus to the Apollo mount, look for a lottery win or another means of coming into money quickly.

The later your fate line begins at the base of the palm, the later you will decide what your work will be. If the fate line is conjoined with the life line at its beginning, it may be hard for you to set yourself up in your chosen career; if your fate line actually begins inside your life line, it means that you have made an incomplete break from your parents and that their influence is holding you back from beginning your public life.

If your fate line originates in the mount of Luna—the area of imagination and sensory input—it may meander a great deal, meaning that you will have several jobs or careers.

Changing Directions

If the fate line changes direction, a change in career situation—if not an entirely new career—may be in store for you. This may mean a promotion or move to a new city for the same employer. A branch from the fate line that goes up adds strength to your career path at that point, and one that goes down represents a setback. Notice where the branch goes to find out more about the kind of influence to expect.

Breaks on your fate line represent changes of direction or transitions in a career. If there is a complete break, you will suffer a change in your financial situation that was inflicted from outside, such as a stock market crash or job layoff. An overlapping break means that you made the decision to make the change at that point in your life, perhaps by choosing a new career. The wider the distance between the breaks, the greater the change. A parallel line next to a break means that you will find the ability to minimize the results of that break through some outside means.

Not all breaks are bad ones. Sometimes changes or transitions can be for the good—you could have been traveling down a path that would have brought you much unhappiness.

Overcoming Obstacles

A cross bar on your fate line represents an obstacle to happiness in your career, such as a difference of opinion at work or a financial worry. Fortunately, such obstacles can be overcome with extra effort. An island on your fate line signals a longer-lasting obstacle that will demand that you find additional patience or else a creative new way around it to overcome the problem.

At the End of the Line

Where your fate line ends is indicative as well of your career's success:

- If your fate line ends at your head line, you may have a crisis in your mid-adult years when you are reassessing your life. At this point, you may be led astray from your intended career path.
- If your fate line continues to your heart line, your career will take its usual route and end in a normal retirement. (A long, straight heart line shows that the owner of the hand is willing to work hard in his or her chosen career.)
- If your fate line continues into the mount of Saturn, you will have an active retirement or perhaps even a second career.
- If your fate line ends in the mount of Jupiter, your career has much to do with your leadership skills or has resulted in high status.

- If your fate line ends between the mounts of Saturn and Apollo, your career involves creativity and will result in fame or financial reward.

The Apollo line is a good indicator of success. If it is strong, you are happy at work and feel rewarded for it. Having many Apollo lines means you are a flexible person and possess many talents. You may change jobs frequently due to boredom.

Finding Your Life's Work

Next, it's time to look at your head line, which can help you with ideas for a career that's right for you. Because it shows your intellectual and mental ability, and how you think, it can give a good idea of the skills you bring to any business undertaking.

There are two kinds of head lines, and each reveals a different personality and skill set. A curved head line shows creativity of thought, and if you have one it means you should look for work in the arts and humanities, perhaps in the media, advertising, or design. It also indicates sensitivity to others. A straight head line, on the other hand, denotes a logical mind of an analytical person who should pursue science, accounting, or engineering. His or her skills will be in working with figures rather than people.

If you have a very long head line, it means you have the ability to focus on your work, indicating you would like a career in pure scientific research or academics, while if you have a shorter head line, you might pursue interests on the practical, hands-on side of life.

Mounting a Career Choice

The mounts of the hand are a second way to see what life work you are best suited for. The mounts show where your energies and talents are stored, and the higher the mount, the more likely you are to have talents in a particular area. A wider mount means that while you do have talent in that area, you are not directing that talent appropriately but squandering it.

The Jupiter Mount

The Jupiter mount is the place to find leadership potential and a sense of justice and authority, so look here if you have plans for a judgeship or want to be a business executive. CEOs typically have square "practical" hands and a large Jupiter mount. An enlarged Jupiter mount also gives a sense of independence and outgoingness, or a "going-against-the-grain" attitude, so many entrepreneurs are square-handed with enlarged Jupiter mounts.

The Saturn Mount

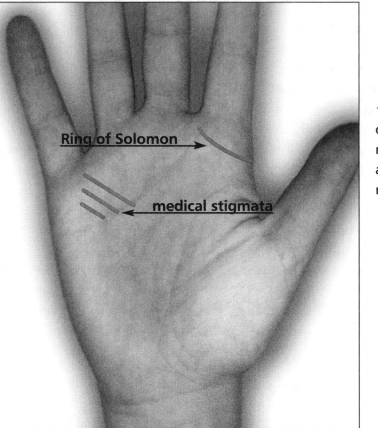

◀ Healing hands often feature medical stigmata and a Solomon ring

The Saturn mount is the repository of wisdom and responsibility. If you have strength in this mount, you will have good research skills and partake in solitary occupations with a more serious purpose, such as a scientist, librarian, cleric, or philosopher. Craftspeople and engineers are also found in this realm. Doctors often have a strong Saturn mount coupled with medical stigmata and a ring of Solomon—which represents wisdom in making good choices for their patients.

The Apollo Mount

The Apollo mount shows creativity, flair, and an aesthetic sense that would lead you to a career in the arts (either fine or applied), or one where you would enjoy public contact, such as advertising or public relations. Other public communicators such as lecturers and receptionists have this mount featured as well. It is interesting to note that most professional writers have deep head lines, along with creative markings on the girdle of Venus and long, thin, and open fingers.

FACT

Stars correctly placed show financial success. On the Jupiter mount, they mean success in life recognized by financial gain. On the Apollo mount, a star means the possessor has some great creative talent that will bring fame as well as fortune. And a star on the Apollo line means that the financial gain will be a result of luck, such as winning a contest.

Mount of Mercury

Mercury is the sign of the communicator and businessperson, so if you have a prominent Mercury mount, you are in good company with teachers, journalists, broadcasters, bankers, salespeople, and lawyers—all of those who must interact well with others. Healthcare workers may also have a prominent Mercury mount.

Luna and Venus

The Luna mount is larger on the hands of those who have a vivid imagination, high sensitivity, and lots of empathy, which are traits favored in many different careers—social work, teaching, health care, art, writing, or music. Look to see if you have travel lines or a life line with a branch toward the Luna mount. If such is the case, being a travel guide or flight attendant would be a good career for you.

Those who have a larger-than-average mount of Venus tend to be very excited about and dedicated to their career. If you have a large Venus mount, choose a profession that requires your completed involvement and dedication.

The Mounts of Mars

If you have a large Lower Mars mount (the mount between the thumb and the mount of Jupiter), you are a person with a great deal of assertiveness and who demonstrates integrity. Becoming an accountant or banker would be good options for you.

If you have a large Upper Mars mount (located under the mount of Mercury), you have courage and fortitude and should consider a job that includes physical competitiveness—you would make a good soldier, athlete, or policeman. Other professions that require physical accomplishments would be well suited as well. These include construction work, farming, and forestry.

A Finger in Every Pie

Once you've had a chance to see what your mounts have to tell you about your life's work, switch your attention to your fingers. They can tell you a lot about yourself, such as how you carry out your duties and use your talents.

Check Your Jupiter Finger

The Jupiter finger is the prime indicator of success in business. Pay careful attention to both the Jupiter finger and its corresponding mount.

Having a straight Jupiter finger shows you are sensible and honest. If it leans outward, you are a financial risk-taker and an adventurer, as well as ambitious. If it leans inward, you are more careful and may even lack confidence in your own ability. The closer the Jupiter finger is to your Saturn finger, the more cautious you are with money. And if your Jupiter finger is longer than the Apollo finger, you are a dominant person and would always seek to do better professionally and promote yourself.

QUESTION?

What does it mean if I have differently shaped fingertips on the fingers of one hand?
If you have differently shaped fingertips, your quest for job satisfaction depends on which finger has what kind of shape. The combination of fingertip and finger will give you information specific to that area of life.

Long middle sections of the finger, the phalanges, show that you have good financial and managerial abilities. If the bottom part of your Jupiter finger has vertical lines, it means you are very organized, but if that is overscored by horizontal lines to form a grille, you can be manipulative in the office environment and like to play politics there.

Measuring Up

Let's go on to see what else your fingers and fingertips can tell about you and career choices. If you have longer fingers, you should choose detail and precision work where speed is not a factor but accurate analysis is. If you have shorter fingers, it is just the opposite—you are a quick thinker, intuitive rather than analytical, and you see the big picture rather than the small details. You are goal-oriented rather than process-oriented.

FACT

If you have a long Mercury finger, you should look for a job in communications, such as a writer, broadcaster, public relations person, or clergyperson.

At Your Fingertips

Your fingertips can tell a lot about the kind of person you are and how you should work:

- **Square:** In general, those with squared fingertips are organized, thorough, and goal-oriented. Secretaries, clerks, and many businesspeople fall into this category.
- **Spatulate:** Those with spatulate fingertips love action and getting things done right away. Many of these people are successful business owners and athletes.
- **Pointed:** Those with pointed fingertips are imaginative and aesthetically oriented, and they have a great sense of idealism.
- **Rounded:** Those with rounded fingertips are indeed well rounded. They can be successful in many different professions and need to look for further guidance in other areas of the hand.

Fingerprinting for Success

Your fingerprints, too, will give you clues as to the right career choice to make. Of course, these remain unchanged by time, but they do give you an idea of what is in your genes that cannot be changed and must be dealt with when it comes to your life work. Take a look at your fingerprints. Do you see any of the following?

- **Arches:** People with fingerprints that are mostly arches are practical and down to earth; they like to work with their hands, whether it be as a surgeon, a mechanic, or a potter.
- **Whorls:** If your fingerprints contain whorls, you are likely to want to specialize in one particular topic and to become renowned for it. You like to work alone so that you can control the work environment and focus on the project at hand, and you tend to be temperamental and innovative.
- **Loops:** Those with fingerprint loops love teamwork and can adapt to many situations. They like the stimulation of changing surroundings and having a lot going on, and they can be either

serious or fun-loving, depending on the type of loop displayed on their fingertips.

- **Composite patterns:** Those with composite fingerprints are good at seeing all points of view, and this makes them good at being arbitrators and jurists.

In any profession, people who have a large mount of Venus will bring a great deal of dedication to the job and sincere concern to those persons with whom the job brings them into contact, outshining any other reward the job may bring.

You can also look at the joints of your fingers to learn more about the attributes you have that will make you valuable in a particular job. If you have knotty joints, you tend to look at things logically and love to do research and solve problems. Think about science, law, or any other rational professional as a career. If you have smooth joints, you use your intuition to make quick assessments, and you like to work with others and to create new projects and ideas of your own rather than studying those of the past.

Getting into Specifics

Certain professions and professional categories are marked by very specific indications on the hand:

- **The teacher's square:** A small square on the Jupiter mount that demonstrates your ability to teach, lecture, or instruct. This is a good sign that your should look to a teaching profession, if not in a school or college, perhaps as a tutor, giver of business or other seminars, football coach, or crafts instructor.
- **The line of Mars:** A sign of courage, the line of Mars is found on the thumb side of the palm between the heart and head lines. Because of what it represents, this is a line that indicates you would have success as a police officer, soldier, fire fighter, or in some other protective

position that requires bravery and a sense of service and duty.

- **The ladder of success:** If you have many lines that run parallel to the fate line near its top, you will get to the top of your professional career—whatever it may be—through hard work and your own efforts.

- **The ring of Solomon:** An arch-shaped line that goes through the Jupiter mount, this ring indicates that you have a propensity toward metaphysical or psychic ability (especially if your hands are marked by the lines of intuition, which begin on the Luna mount and swerve upward to the mount of Mercury), or that you are interested in people and have deep insights about their motivations and desires. In this case, therapy or psychology are good career options for you. Often, those with a ring of Solomon have good leadership skills and excel at managing other people by appealing to their nature.

- **The medical stigmata:** A series of at least three tiny vertical lines above the heart line on the Mercury mount, where the Mercury (health) line ends. This marking indicates that you have an interest in the healing professions, and you might want to explore life as a physician, medical technician, nurse, or massage therapist.

Hiring Hands: Choosing Good Employees

Many human resources people depend on a variety of tests to choose the right employees for their company. These tests may measure skills, such as math or typing, or they may be psychological and creativity tests. If you work in human resources, or if you are in a position to be hiring employees, you might also want to use some of the concepts behind palmistry to get a better idea of a candidate's mental and psychological fitness for the job.

While interviewing job candidates, look especially at the shape of the hand, the length and shape of the fingers, and evaluate how firm the handshake is; these are all good indicators of general character and can give you a quick read of a person without the necessity of reading each line on their hands.

Chapter 16

Your Lifeline to Good Health

Health means far more than just the absence of illness. To be healthy means being in a positive state physically, mentally, and socially. Health is determined by many things: heredity, environment (which includes the people and things that surround us), and the way we interact and deal with our environment. Our minds and bodies are linked by the chemicals in the brain, and the lines of the hands showcase our internal workings both physically and psychologically.

Assessing Your Health

There are many areas of the hand that you can look at in order to assess your health. First, let's look at the most obvious signs—temperature, color, texture, and musculature of the hand. All of these, if studied together, can give you a good idea of the basic state of a person's health.

FACT

Just as our health is largely determined by the physiologies we inherit from our ancestors, so are our fingerprints—and handprints. Handprints for the members of a family share many common features and characteristics. By looking at similarities in the hand, you can trace similarities of character, personality, or interest.

Coloring and Temperature

The palms should be pinkish in persons of all races. Pale skin and pale creases can mean that the person is in an extremely worrisome situation or else lacks iron, perhaps, in the case of women, due to particularly heavy menstruation. A reddish cast over the outside of the palm may mean that a woman is pregnant, while yellowish hands can mean a liver disease or else a diet that is heavy in carrots.

"Cold hands, warm heart" is not always the case. A person with cold hands may have circulatory problems, and if the hand is both cold and damp, they may be worried or suffer from insomnia. The best evidence of allergies and circulatory problems comes in the form of islands, grilles, and vertical lines along the three major lines of the hands. Cold, pale hands also indicate lack of energy.

With very cold hands, look for a bluish color on the nails that signifies poor circulation. Hands that are warm and bluish also indicate poor circulation and pulmonary problems, and perhaps even a negative reaction to a drug.

Very red skin on the hands can mean circulatory problems that include high blood pressure or diabetes. Hot, red hands can mean rheumatic fever, gout, or a glandular problem, or they can indicate an angry temperament.

It is important to note that what you see in the hand is only an indication that you are vulnerable in a certain area. It does not mean that you have a particular disease or condition—it may be there as a warning.

The Texture of the Skin

Skin texture is important because it is controlled by the hormones, the chemicals produced by the endocrine system, which controls such personality-related traits as mood swings. In general, soft and fine skin means the person is sensitive and vulnerable, while coarser skin means that he or she is robust and protected from disease.

Skin texture can also indicate specific health problems. Dry and rough skin is a warning of an underactive thyroid, while smooth and satiny hands show an overactive thyroid, as do soft and pudgy fingers.

Minor hand lines are often the result of stress and worry, which in turn can cause disease. Oddly, the fewer lines appear on your hand, the more balanced, peaceful, and healthy you are.

Muscle Elasticity

You can also learn a lot about your health simply by examining how your hands feel—whether they have good musculature and are elastic. If they are, you are likely able to resist illness; when you do get sick, you recover quickly. Incidentally, people with elastic hands are generally adaptable to new ideas and unanticipated problems.

A soft and doughy feeling to the hand's fleshy parts means a similar softness, a lack of resilience, in the physical constitution. People with soft hands are often too indulgent when it comes to eating, drinking, resting, and sex. This is particularly the case in people with thick hands. People with thin and weak hands tend to lack vitality and endurance and they are prone to illness and nutritional problems.

A rigid hand with mounts that are hard and inflexible means that the owner of the hand is rigid and unyielding as well. This characteristic shows that the person might eventually develop stress-related physical problems such as cardiovascular difficulties, back pain, headaches, and ulcers that are caused by holding in emotions and stored energies. These people need to find healthy outlets for their emotions, such as exercise.

To test your muscular consistency, try this: Make a fist of your hand and press your thumb against your Apollo finger. Look at the muscle behind your thumb. If it is firm, your ability to withstand illness is probably good. If it is soft, you may be low in energy. If this muscle appears to be atrophying, it could mean you have diabetes.

The Shape of Healthy Hands

The shape of your hand is another good indicator of what kinds of health conditions may affect you. Following is a rundown of the basic hand types, with an idea of the health conditions that their owners should look out for and guidelines to help them avoid the problems that are most likely to plague them:

- Air-handed people should be aware that they are vulnerable to respiratory problems such as asthma and colds. Because they think and worry all the time, they also have a tendency to nervous conditions and can easily tire themselves out and run themselves ragged with frenzied anxiety. Those with air hands should avoid smoking and learn to relax, both physically and mentally.
- Earth-handed people may eat and drink too much and too quickly, in which case they are likely to have digestive problems. They need to watch their diets and to learn to exercise often, both to help control the weight and to work off stress and anxiety. Their love of the outdoors will help them achieve this goal.
- Fire-handed people like to burn their candles at both ends; they need to slow down and relax so as to avoid heart and circulatory problems. The speed that these people live at also makes them prone

to accidents; they must learn that careful and deliberate action is much safer and just as productive.

• Water-handed people are extremely sensitive and have a vulnerable psyche, so they are at risk for depression, addiction, and other mental illnesses. They should take extreme care to avoid overindulgence in plumbing the psychological depths. They are also vulnerable in areas that relate to the immune system, such as arthritis and allergy.

E ALERT!

Always remember that if your hand gives you an indication of future problems, you can heed the warning and avoid illness by eating better, getting more exercise and sleep, giving up unhealthy habits such as smoking, and getting timely medical attention.

Calling on Your Life Line

Another vital indicator of a person's physical and mental health status is found in the lines and patterns of the palms. These develop on the fetus in the second trimester and therefore are central to your well-being. They show your energy levels, emotional balance, and ability to overcome pain and illness. They will help you see what conditions are likely to bother you before they show up in other areas of the body. This lets you take preventive measures and work to build up your health in those problem areas.

Of course, the first place to look on the palm to assess the state of your general health is the life line, which can tell you a lot if you examine its length, depth, and legibility. All people have a life line, and it is the first line that appears on the hand of the newly developing baby. Its span—from between your thumb and Jupiter finger and swooping around the mount of Venus to your wrist—encompasses your entire life and represents, among other things, your health—illnesses, accidents, emotional traumas, and weaknesses. A long, deep, unobstructed life line signifies that you have a strong and healthy body that can fight off disease and recover quickly from accidents.

Marks of Vulnerability

When it comes to marks that appear around your life line, here are the ones that carry clues about your health:

- **Breaks:** A break in the line at a certain point in time may represent a major operation or serious illness.
- **Stars:** These may signal injury or a surgical procedure.
- **Islands:** Times when your health is jeopardized and you are more vulnerable to illness. If they are shaped like oblong blobs, you may have a predisposition to cancer.
- **Colored dot:** This mark could indicate a high fever; if the heart or head line shows a similar dot in the area around the same period of time, you may be looking at when a particular disease is due to set in.
- **Diamond:** Indicates gynecological or urological troubles.

Your life line can be strengthened by two other lines. There could be an inner life line that goes alongside the main line; this line can fortify the main life line and provide additional support in times of need. The same is true of your fate line, which runs in close parallel to the life line for most of your life.

Heading Toward Health

Your head line contains health-related clues for you as well. When you are concerned about health matters, a long head line can mean hyperactivity and behavioral problems.

If you've got a small reddish or brownish group of lines near your mount of Luna, it could signify trouble with your bladder or kidneys. Start drinking lots of water or cranberry juice, and watch those lines disappear!

A fuzzy area on your head line signals a time of mental strain. During times such as these, make sure to relax and to get enough sleep. A star that appears on the head line warns of a possible head injury. Small indentations when the hand is stretched can represent migraines. A branch dropping out of the head line can indicate depression.

Healthy Heart Line, Healthy Heart

As you might expect, the heart line is an extremely good indicator of the health of your cardiovascular system and your emotional disturbances. Indeed, the heart line covers both the physical areas and the realms of passion, so please do not interpret any break or anomaly on it solely as a medical condition. Look to your physician to do that for you.

With that in mind, you can check the heart line for breaks, islands, or dots that give you a warning about your heart or emotional health. A star can represent a heart attack, as can a break or fragmenting, and marks on the heart line below the Apollo finger can mean a calcium imbalance or insomnia. Small lines above the heart line but below the Apollo and Mercury fingers can mean dental problems. When the head and heart line coincide to form the simian line, you should be sure to look for coronary problems.

Reading Your Health Line

The Mercury line, also called the health line, begins at the life line and rises toward the Mercury mount. If you have this line—not everyone does—you may have a problem with gastrointestinal or liver diseases. This line can also indicate kidney problems and problems with the uterus and ovaries, especially if it is weak and broken. In conjunction with yellowish skin, a weak Mercury line may signal liver disease; together with breaks on the heart line, it warns of emotional restrictions that can lead to gastrointestinal distress.

Via Lascivia

While you are in this area, you should also look at the via lascivia, a minor line that runs below and alongside the Mercury line from the life line upward. Formerly thought to indicate excessive interest and overindulgence in sex, it is now believed to show sensitivity to foods and other substances and so indicates allergies and addictions.

FACT

The bracelets around the wrist, called rascettes, are traditional indicators of a long life, depending on how many lines there are—the deeper and stronger they are, the healthier the person. However, an arch in the topmost rascette can signal gynecological problems and perhaps even difficultly in childbearing.

Unfortunately, some of the substances that the via lascivia pinpoints as problematic are drugs—both legal and illegal—and alcohol, tobacco, and caffeine. If you have this line, pay special attention to moderate use of any legal substances (if you use them at all), and, of course, stay away from the illegal ones.

Fingers and Fingertips

A third place to look at health in the hands, beyond the hand itself and the lines on it, are the fingers and fingertips (both the padded tips on one side and the nails on the other). First, begin with the fingers, because every finger is representative of a particular part of the body or facet of life.

In general, horizontal lines across the fingertips are lines that indicate that the aspect of that finger is "crossed" or blocked. For instance, lines across the Jupiter finger, the seat of control and power, show worry about the self and its potency. Lines across the Saturn finger mean you are worried about your home and safety issues. Lines across the Apollo finger indicate that there is a bar to fulfillment—something is making you sad. And lines across the Mercury finger show a problem with communication, either verbally or sexually.

The Endocrine Glands

Lines that go vertically along the fingers have something else to say, and it involves the body's system of endocrine glands. On the Jupiter finger, these lines refer to problems with the pituitary gland; on the Saturn finger, with the pineal gland; on the Apollo finger, with the thymus gland, cardiovascular system, and blood pressure; and on the Mercury finger, with the thyroid.

Nailing Your Diagnosis

The fingernails are another essential part of reading physical and mental health, and their link to health is totally substantiated. Physicians generally use the nails to look for physical problems such as circulatory diseases, iron deficiency, and glandular illnesses.

Just as it is with the skin, the color of the nails is a good way to assess health. Fingernails should be smooth and pink, which shows good nutrition and a healthy outlook. If nails are red, there may be high blood pressure, or you may experience inability to control anger and other emotions. Those with bluish nails may have circulatory problems; they may also lack warmth in their relations with other people. In dealing with both circulatory and emotional problems, exercise and other activity that is approved by your doctor can help improve blood flow and release pent-up emotions in a healthy manner.

ALERT!

A soft, pinkish mount of Luna on the hand of a woman can indicate a pregnancy. Often, this characteristic can appear well before the pregnancy test results are positive!

Like pale skin, pale nails may mean poor eating habits and lack of energy, while yellow skin and nails can indicate liver disease. Brown nails are another sign of poor eating habits, or perhaps problems with the nervous system, and gray fingernails show that the person has malaria.

White spots on your nails are signs of tiredness and worry, and may show that you have a long-standing depression, or an imbalance of zinc.

If they are also soft, you could lack calcium in your diet. In general, soft nails show poor eating habits and a diet lacking in protein, and they can indicate arthritis. Nails that break easily show an endocrine system imbalance.

If you have moons on all your fingers, you are in good health and likely to remain so. If you are totally lacking moons, and your nails are in poor condition, you may have an underactive thyroid, but if your moons fill over a third of your nail, your thyroid could be overactive.

Nail Shapes and What They Signal

The shape of your nails can also tell you a great deal about the state of your health:

- **Fan-shaped or very narrow nails:** You have a nervous condition or psychological disturbance such as extreme impatience or jumpiness.
- **Short nails:** You have very high expectations of others and of your life, and may have depression or circulatory illnesses.
- **Concave nails:** Nails that turn up at the ends show dietary shortcomings such as anemia, dermatological problems, and an underactive thyroid.
- **Clubbed nails or those with bluish bases:** You are vulnerable to heart disease or a lung disorder. This is especially true if the nails are also shaped like a watch crystal and they wrap around the fingertip. In this case, also look for respiratory diseases.

Lines and ridges on the nails are extremely important in reading for health issues. Long longitudinal ridges can be the result of chronic illnesses such as dermatological disorders, rheumatic conditions, intestinal problems, and hyperthyroidism. Deep vertical ridges that rise up from the base of the nail to the tip as it develops can mean that a person has suffered a trauma such as an emotional shock, dietary deprivation, a bad infection, or some other physical stressor. If there are lines instead of deep ridges, there has been arsenic poisoning, a high fever, or a heart problem.

A "Handy" Exercise

Many of the health problems that can be discovered by an examination of the hand can be improved by relaxation. Getting a hand massage is a great way to help someone relax and a good way to end a palm reading. It also helps control pain, soothes the psyche, diminishes circulatory problems, and improves muscle tone. You can also give yourself a hand massage any time you have a free minute, especially after you have been using your hands at a particular task, such as typing.

Following are a series of steps for giving a good hand massage:

1. Press your thumb across the base of the hand to loosen it up. Then press down and massage the fleshy areas of the mounts. Use firm pressure to stimulate the circulation and make sure your movements go toward the heart.
2. After that, massage each finger and the thumb from tip to palm on both sides.
3. Pinch the tip of each finger and the thumb and manipulate it from side to side and back to front to relax the hand and improve dexterity.
4. Stroke the tendons on the back of the hand to relax them, and then rub the webs of the hand between the thumb and each of the fingers.
5. Pull down on the fingers as a unit to increase wrist tension, and then release it. Pull up to bend the wrist the other way.
6. Interlace your hands and stretch them out to release tension and flex the fingers repeatedly.
7. Finally, shake your hands to improve the circulation.

ESSENTIAL

Remember that the lines of the palm are changing, and that following good health habits and seeking timely medical intervention can change the indications of poor health found on the hand to ones of strength and vigor.

Exercises like this—as well as aerobic exercise, getting enough rest, good eating habits, healthy relationships, and finding a good emotional balance—can go a long way toward improving your health or keeping yourself hale and whole. Remember that all of these indications show possibilities and potential, and that diagnosis should be based on many different features and cannot be substantiated without confirmation by a physician.

Chapter 17

The Places You'll Go

All of life is a journey, and the adventures you undertake in that journey are written on your hand. All travels, whether it is an around-the-world jaunt, a move to a new town, the decision to join the Peace Corps—or even the movement from employment to retirement—will leave their mark on your palm. These marks can also be used to give you an idea of what you will face on the road and help you become a wiser and better-prepared traveler.

Travel in the Palm of Your Hand

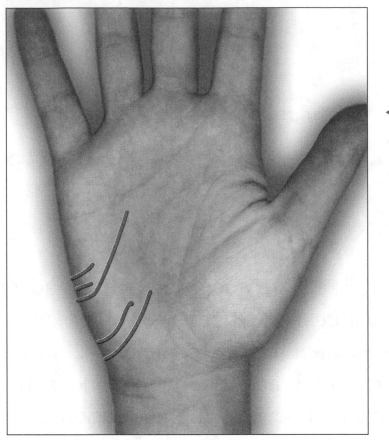

◀ Travel lines

The most obvious way to start your exploration is to see if you have any travel lines. These lines generally begin at the bottom of the percussion, by the rascette, and extend across your palm, crossing over the mount of Luna, and perhaps extending upward to the heart line. If strong, they sometimes extend all the way across the palm to the mount of Venus. Travel lines represent journeys of discovery, adventure, or healing.

Each of the small travel lines extending from the heel represents a journey, so they can be read individually. The longer and stronger the line, the more influential that particular trip will be over the course of your life. The lower on the hand the travel lines are, the more likely travel will be a growth experience. Travel lines originating higher indicate more problematic travel.

QUESTION?

Is travel important?
It's good to remember that the importance of travel to the individual whose palm is being read, as seen in the depth and length of the travel lines, is relative. One deep travel line may mean a great deal to someone who travels little but makes one major journey, perhaps to college or a new home. But to someone who travels often, each individual trip may be of lesser importance and may be seen in smaller, lighter lines.

The presence of one heavy travel line that goes far shows that you will travel often, whether on major adventures, on business trips, or moving the home for work or family, but always for substantial reasons that will affect your life. However, if you have a series of lighter lines, you may be traveling a lot but taking smaller trips and vacations that have little influence over your life as a whole.

Happy Trails

All of life is a journey, and the markings of the palm are important guides in this journey. But this is especially true when you travel outside of your home and town, leaving behind your usual support system and venturing into the unknown. Travel brings discovery and growth, but it is also a time to be especially wary and careful, and good guidance is essential. The things learned through palmistry can be a valuable lodestar for the traveler setting out on a journey, for the hand has much to tell us.

Like the other lines of the hand, travel lines can be intersected, and the lines intersecting them will tell their own story. If your travel line crosses your life line at a certain point, this shows that your trip will be made for reasons of health. It may be a trip to a more healthful area, a stay in an out-of-town hospital for treatment, or a visit to a spa for recuperation and healing. If the travel line crosses the fate line, it shows a trip that will improve the life of the individual in ways involving career, security, and responsibility.

ALERT!

If you have a heavy deep travel line on the mount of Luna, you probably love to travel—but beware. This line warns of daring, adventurous, or downright dangerous behavior, so avoid taking risks, whether they are physical or emotional, when you are traveling away from home.

Travelers by Hand Type

Are you an adventuresome world traveler or a person who prefers to stay close to home? What is going to be your final destination? Even if you are not sure, the shape of your hand can let you know. The information your hands contain can show what kind of traveler you are and how you approach your voyage through life—your general propensity toward travel and attitude toward it. Here are the interpretations for each of the hand shapes:

- **Earth-handed:** As you might expect, people with earth hands like to stay at home and enjoy what they know and what is familiar to them. When they do travel, they visit outdoor destinations where they can enjoy and partake of nature and the elements. They tend to take their vacations in the countryside rather than in the city, and they like to revisit the same places year after year, because they know what makes them happy.
- **Water-handed:** People with water hands are attracted to places of mystery, power, and spiritual growth. They enjoy exploring ancient sites and historical monuments that convey a sense of time's passage and give an idea of how our ancestors lived, worked, and thought. They are also drawn to activities of aesthetic appreciation—concerts, museums, theater festivals, and art fairs—where they can enjoy humanity's highest expressions of creativity.
- **Fire-handed:** People with fire hands are adventurous and love to explore new places and discover new ideas and cultures. They are like children, ever running forward to seek the unknown, always excited about seeing what is around the next bend.

- **Air-handed:** People with air hands enjoy travel the most. They like the stimulation of interacting with other cultures, learning about diverse people and places, comparing and contrasting destinations, and exchanging their ideas about it all with their new friends. Plus, they love to be the ones in the know about where to go and what to do, what's to be seen and where to see it.

Warnings and Danger Signs

Now that you know what kind of a traveler you are, it's time to read the warning signs displayed on your palm. As with any other line, the interpretation of a travel line is subject to other markings:

- Overlaps and breaks on the travel line indicate that travel will be delayed at that point.
- Bars and other lines that cross the travel line show obstacles to travel and interferences that you must overcome.
- A star on the travel line is an indication that there could be danger or disaster ahead—perhaps a train or car accident, or problems with delays caused by a faulty aircraft. Look to your life line to see if there is a corresponding star in the same frame as the journey to see how much cause there is for concern.
- An island on a travel line means a traveler should beware, because the trip may have an entirely unanticipated and nasty end, such as bad travel connections that leave you stranded, getting lost in unfamiliar territory, or not being able to achieve the goals of the trip. It could even be as serious as a dangerous result, say becoming the victim of a crime.
- A square on the travel line adds protection for the traveler at the point where it appears.

Problems with travel may not just mean car accidents or lost luggage. They can also show that the trip does not meet its intended goal: a bad sales call or dissatisfying move to a new town.

The Prospect of Relocation

Relocation—finding a new place to live and work—is perhaps the ultimate form of travel. It means tearing yourself and your family away from the familiar and comfortable and journeying toward a new life in which the outcome is unknown. Anyone facing such a challenge will need all the help that a reading can give about the outcome of such an event, and to find ways to minimize obstacles and problems while preparing for the journey. Relocating can mean anything from a move down the street to beginning a new life on a new continent, so there are many things to consider when you are facing relocation.

Check Your Major Lines

The kind of movement represented by relocation is found on the palm, not so much in the travel lines on the percussion of the hand but rather along the life line and its branches. The information given in this area can be expanded by looking at other areas of the palm as well.

For example, if your relocation means buying and selling property in preparation for moving your household, it is important to look at your Saturn mount, since this is where issues dealing with home and security can best be studied. A branch moving forward from the life line to this area would indicate the possibility of a major move and give you some idea about the effect the move will have on you. A move made for reasons of health will be seen by a branch from the life line, which represents the physical area, to the Luna mount.

Changing Continents

But what if the move is more than a move across town to a new neighborhood? A farther move—say, immigrating to a new country to make a fresh start or to study a new culture—is a much larger under-taking. This type of a change will be marked on the Luna mount. This is where foreign travel shows up in the hand, so any overseas relocation or a long journey in foreign parts will be obvious here.

People who enjoy travel have a life line that takes up a good portion of the palm and leaves a large mount of Venus. Those who do not like travel have a life line close to the wrist and circling toward the thumb, leaving a smaller mount of Venus.

A New Beginning

The end of the career is a move as well—away from job responsibilities and security to new opportunities and vistas. While the movement to retired status is a journey in and of itself, a time to learn about yourself and grow in many ways, it is also a time when people become more free to travel and explore new places and ideas. Therefore, retirement can be seen as an exciting and productive time in life, as change brings growth; it is always beneficial to prepare yourself as much as possible for any change, and especially one as life-altering as retirement, by learning all you can about what awaits you. This is why retirement is often a time when many people hope to seek new insights and gain guidance from palmistry.

The transition from a working life in public to a private life in retirement is seen in the fate line. But not everyone retires late in life, so look for other financial and lifestyle cues.

The three areas of the palm that are most affected by retirement are the fate line, the Apollo line, and last section of the life line, and this is where you should concentrate your reading when helping those facing retirement.

The Life Line

The life line involves your physical well-being, ability to withstand change, and enthusiasm for life, so it is a central part of any reading concerning retirement. This can be seen as especially true when you realize that the life line also involves motivation, family relationships, and lifestyle, major elements that need to be considered when a person is making the move to retirement.

Look at the latter part of the life line to note the part that reflects your retirement experiences. The clearer this area, the better an experience with retirement you can expect. A strong new path for the life line after retirement should mean an improved life, with new interests and goals, or at least more time to pursue the old ones.

Several new branches coming out of your life line in the area after retirement represent your journeys or visits. If your life line divides at the base and one end points to the Luna mount, you will leave your birthplace and live abroad. However, an island here would indicate that you will have health problems or other long-term frustrations of well-being associated with retirement.

Because your life line in general shows events involving family and interpersonal conflicts, as well as your ability to endure and stay on course, any problem you can see on the life line in this area could be interpreted as a problem with your spouse or with finding something useful to do after the career ends. Often, the end of a career throws a married couple more closely together than ever before, while at the same time it dissolves a sense of structure and old routines, so retirement can cause a great deal of family stress.

The Apollo Line

The Apollo line indicates a successful outcome and it develops from satisfaction in what you have done. Because the Apollo line represents personal fulfillment, its appearance at the time of your retirement is indicative of how successful your retirement will be. The stronger and more definite your Apollo line, as it lies above the heart line, the better your retirement period can be expected to be. A good Apollo line shows that the person has arrived at some sense of accomplishment, and has reached a goal long sought after.

Traditionally, if there seem to be a set of parallel Apollo lines above the heart line, it indicates a certain financial stability. If you go by this traditional interpretation, the more lines appear, the more money there will be.

The Apollo line signifies retirement and usually is a short line, beginning above the heart line and running to the Apollo finger. It reveals the ability to adapt to the new challenges of retirement and loss of status and structure.

The Fate Line

The fate line is vital to the study of the hand, as it indicates the overall structure of life, the focus that guides our efforts and the conscious expression of what we hold dear. The upper part of the fate line is the one most involved in studying the topics of retirement. Because of its overall prominence in depicting the direction a life takes, changes in the fate line there are especially important when considering retirement.

A break in the fate line, with a continuation, could show an early retirement. If the fate line branches at this time or continues in many directions, it shows an expansion of life interests. However, the presence of an island at the end of your fate line can mean you will be frustrated in the financial area, with the shortage of income during that time suggested by the length of the island.

Retirement covers many aspects of life: health, finance, travel, and new growth chief among them. It is important to be careful and thorough when doing a reading about retirement, as so many interrelated aspects are involved.

A Handy Retirement

Just as it does in other areas, the shape of your hand will give you an indication of the kind of retirement you will prefer. Persons with the different hand shapes will approach retirement differently, believing that they are giving up certain things by leaving the workplace and finding that they can compensate for their losses with new activities after retirement. Here are some general reading guidelines:

- **Air-handed:** Those with air hands will miss the exchange of ideas in the workplace, the energy of productivity, and the sense of keeping up with new information. They can replace this feeling during retirement by taking courses to meet their interests so that they can learn something new, and by taking care to stay connected to colleagues and others in their field for intellectual stimulation.
- **Fire-handed:** Fire-handed people will miss the congeniality of the workplace and the sense of belonging to be found there. They can replace this feeling during retirement through volunteer and community work, by joining clubs and other associations so that they can develop new relationships, and by traveling to see family and friends.
- **Earth-handed:** Earth-handed people will miss the stability and reassurance of the workplace, with its known patterns, but they can replace this feeling during retirement by establishing new patterns and rituals in life. They should also make sure to spend part of every day close to the earth, gardening, or walking in the woods.
- **Water-handed:** People will enjoy being free of the constraints and bustle of the workplace, and while they enjoy the quiet of retirement, they can replace the creativity they put into their work life with creative pastimes at home, such as art, music, and crafts work.

ALERT!

Generally, retirement lies near the end of life. People who are retiring may be concerned about death, either their own or that of their partner. While palmistry cannot predict a death, it can uncover anxiety about health matters that can be dealt with by looking closely at other lines.

Whatever the shape of your hand, you can be guided to a better experience with retirement by noting what the lines of your hand have to say about it. And this is true of all the other journeys in life we take as well, be they a short vacation to Niagara Falls or a relocation to Tibet or Belize. Ⓔ

Chapter 18

Lines and Patterns of Your Spiritual Compass

Your hands can tell you about the quality of your life and relationships with others, but they can also offer insight into your spirituality—your spiritual path in this life and its connection to the universe. Like beacons of light, the lines and markings of your hand can even serve as your guides, pointing you in the right direction when you're certain you've lost all hope.

The Hand-Spirit Connection

In almost every religious or spiritual belief system, hands play a critical role in expression of spirit. They are just as meaningful clapping to a Baptist gospel song as they are in the healing sessions in the esoteric fields such as reiki. They can be folded in prayer, offer blessings in the form of hand positions such as the Buddhist mudra or peace blessing, or can be placed over the head of a small child in a baptism.

ESSENTIAL

You can use palmistry as a mirror into your soul, to help you discover your life's path and to create meaning and joy in your life. Your lines can help you connect with your sacred self.

In palmistry, all religions are represented and respected, and lines are read according to each individual's personal belief system. Since palmistry itself is not a religion, it allows for a wide spectrum of religious expression to be played out in the lines of your hand.

Where Energy Flows . . . the Lines Will Go

Lines can represent the flow of energy in your physical body, but that energy also drives spirituality, helping to fuel the belief systems that propel you into the future, giving you the strength and passion to grow your spiritual self. When your hands touch anything, but especially another human being's hands, there is an almost electrical charge of energy that is exchanged. Spend a moment or two touching hands with another person you're close to, and note the energy that transpires!

In reiki, which is a simple laying of hands that creates a healing exchange of energy between two or more people, the energy is believed to be of an active, healing nature—and after years of regular practice, reiki practitioners often report a deepening of their lines and more pronounced Jupiter mounts; this is proof that extending your spiritual self can indeed change the patterns, lines, and mounts of your palm over time.

Many reiki practitioners and psychic healers have the same basic hand shape as doctors, nurses, and others in the more traditional healing professions. These are the pointed (psychic) hands, slender and with pointed fingers.

Your Spiritual Future

One of the greatest outcomes of a palm reading is the insight into your inner self—but not only do your lines tell you where you've been, they also tell you where you might be going, particularly from a spiritual standpoint.

That's not to say that lines and mounts can predict whether you're Protestant, Catholic, Buddhist, or Muslim, but they can indicate how deep your spiritual conviction is, and whether it is likely to be more traditional or nontraditional in nature. The aim of all palmistry is to unlock secrets, heal old patterns and hurts, and move forward into a future filled with possibility and renewal—a process that truly couldn't be more spiritual in nature, since the essence of spiritual life is to get in touch with your Higher Self in order to evolve to the next level of consciousness, however you choose to define its ultimate meaning and applicability to your life.

Finding Your Spiritual Center

With all of the many lines and patterns on your hands, it may at first seem difficult to sort through it all to find your "spiritual center." Where, in all the lines, is your spiritual path? What is your true calling in life, and how can you best answer that call in a practical, "hands-on" manner? The best thing to do is to start with the most dominant feature of the hand pertaining to spiritual matters—the prayerful mount of Jupiter.

The Prayer Mount

The Jupiter mount represents not only our leadership abilities, but also the ability to communicate with a "higher leader." In most cases, this mount is located right between the head and heart lines, directly beneath the Jupiter or index finger. In palmistry, this area is considered the "spiritual central," since it represents our overall tendency to believe in a higher power or a higher level of consciousness. Some say the mount of Jupiter actually represents our belief in the power of miracles.

ESSENTIAL

Small, diagonal lines across the bottom part of the Luna mount can reveal extrasensory perception, or ESP. If you have these rare lines, you have an uncanny ability to "see" things before they happen.

A well-developed Jupiter mount indicates a deeply spiritual and devout person—someone who believes in the power of the unseen and who doesn't rely on scientific proof with respect to spiritual matters. An underdeveloped mount can indicate a person whose spirituality manifests itself in the material rather than the ethereal world—this person worships at the great gift shop of life rather than drinking from the well of souls. This is not a desirable configuration.

The Shape of Spirit

Most deeply spiritual people have psychic or pointed hands, with long, narrow fingers and narrow palms. These are the metaphysically or intuitively inclined, and many of these types are also writers or speakers on metaphysical topics.

Does this mean that the square-handed aren't as gifted? Yes—and no. The square-handed have a more earthy or practical spirituality, and are more akin to nature-based American Indian spirituality. They worship the earthly creations of Spirit, preferring to have spiritual communion with the plants and animals along the dusty path of their lives. They have both feet on the ground, quite literally, and are not given to verbal pronouncements of spirituality. They are quiet, content, and peaceful believers.

People with rounded hands are easygoing followers—they are typically very concerned with walking the straight and narrow, and are very morally correct in their words and actions. They can be trustworthy friends and are good, caring listeners.

ALERT!

A narrow gap between the heart and head lines can signify a closed mind, while a wide gap can mean you're too open-minded and likely to be very nontraditional in your personal belief system.

Those with mixed hand shapes are often the most open-minded of the spiritual set, and they may even take pride in having their own, hybrid brand of religion. They have a tendency to take whatever they consider to be the best from every religious belief system and leave the rest for others to sort through. They are progressive thinkers and sometimes even start their own churches.

Zoning Out

In Chapter 3, we looked at the divisions of the hand, splitting it into four quadrants or zones. The zone closest to the mount of Luna was identified as the physical, or intuitive, zone—and it is the zone most often examined in a spiritually focused reading because this area indicates how responsive and receptive you are intuitively, but also physically to your surroundings.

A dominant physical/intuitive zone points to an acutely sensitive personality of those who are able to quickly assess people and situations on a deeply intuitive level. When these people have a "feeling" about anything, others should listen up! Of course, if this area of the hand is not well developed, it means that the individual is more grounded and even rationally minded.

Unique Markings on Your Spiritual Path

When doing a spiritually oriented reading, most of your time will be spent close to the mount of Jupiter. Once you've looked at the overall appearance of the mount, you'll also want to look for any uniquely shaped markings.

For instance, you might see a grille-shaped marking on the Jupiter mount, and this would mean a need to make sense of everything you process in your heart and spirit. For you, traditional religion holds too many mysteries, leaving you feeling disconnected from others in your spiritual community. It would be helpful for you to seek the advice of a good spiritual leader to help you sort through the "noise" in your head and get some clarity. Remember, you can't be one with the universe without getting clear about your inner voice first.

While it sounds ominous, a cross on your Jupiter mount can actually be fortuitous; it can mean you have a magnetic way of drawing people in to your deepest spiritual thoughts—and can lead interesting groups that delve deeply into spiritual exploration. You have charisma and could make a good living as a chaplain, minister, or other spiritual leader.

A star portends a healthy, full-of-vitality attitude and is a positive sign except in cases where there is more than one star. In the rare case there are more stars on the mount, you should be careful not to let your personal ambitions drive your spirituality—too much power can mislead you and others onto the wrong paths. Be careful to include the thoughts and concerns of others in your group discussions—and be grateful for their input.

E ALERT!

A wide space between your head and life lines means you are an independent spirit. When these two lines are closely linked together, it can mean you are shy and easily led by others' beliefs, making you more of a spiritual "follower."

Chains are not as healthy a sign to have on your hands in terms of spirituality because they tend to hold you back from your life potential. If you have chains near your Jupiter mount, you may find that you are always dependent on others to lead you out of temptation, so to speak, and into the light. Pray for guidance and strength to overcome any spiritual barriers that hold you back from feeling healthy and complete.

Circles on the Jupiter mount typically belong to the religious hypocrites—those who don't practice what they preach and have a "holier-than-thou" attitude. Steer clear of these folks, as they can be extremely judgmental.

Lines and Loops of Special Meaning

There are several specific lines and patterns you should look for on your hands as indicators of where you are on your spiritual path:

- **Line of Solomon:** This line, which is located directly across the mount of Jupiter, is especially important for wisdom and empathy. If it is dominant, it points to unusually pronounced empathy for others. If it is smooth, however, it means you have only an ordinary level of empathy and are more of a good listener than a giver of advice.
- **Empathy loop:** This loop, located above the rascette toward the middle of the palm, is specifically found on the hands of the great humanitarians. These are the people who take on the problems of the world easily, and who offer big shoulders for just about anyone who needs support.
- **Fate line:** Your destiny or fate line indicates your direction in life and the level of responsibility you are willing to take for your spiritual choices.
- **Apollo line:** This line, which runs diagonally, indicates the degree of emotional and spiritual fulfillment in your life. If it is fine and thin, you may still be exploring your more spiritual side; perhaps taking classes would be of help to you in making the choices that bring you greater fulfillment.
- **Simian line:** The presence of this line can mean an abrupt shift in religious affiliation, particularly to something very unorthodox. If the line is deep, it can portend affiliation with a religious cult.
- **Samaritan lines:** Not all people have them, but when they do, samaritan lines appear along the Mercury mount. They not only point to those in the healing professions, but also to any well-rounded, highly interesting people who are often quite knowledgeable about

many different spiritual belief systems, and are quite conversant about the esoteric.

- **Girdle of Venus:** Always pertaining to emotional life, the girdle of Venus represents your degree of sensitivity. Are you too sensitive? If so, regular mineral sea salts are recommended to "call" your energy back; too often, the highly sensitive or intuitive put out too much of their own energy to help others, and this is something the lines on your hands can register as weakness (in the form of weak lines). If your girdle of Venus is strong, you are likely good at balancing that energy.

A triangle, particularly on the mount of Luna, points to a person with tremendous wisdom and creativity. If you have this marking, you are doubly blessed!

You should also look at your relationship lines to see how well you can relate to others in a listening and sharing capacity. Do you have the ability to reach others at a heart level—can you positively affect their lives in a way that empowers them to make meaningful change? If your relationship lines are strong and deep, you are indeed blessed with the ability and, most likely mission, to help others who are in a state of spiritual need. You have the healing touch.

Karmic Connections

One of the more common questions in advanced palmistry is whether the soul actually imprints the lines in our hands with the messages carried over from a previous life. In other words, do certain life lessons, if left unlearned in a past life, show up as our major challenges in this life and are charted on our hands?

It is indeed possible for some hands to show unfinished business from a previous life. For instance, if in a previous life you were very selfish and materialistic, these tendencies may show up in this life's hands as a warning sign to you. Perhaps your awareness of such behavior or tendencies could bring about positive change early on in this life—and as your behavior changes, so will the lines on your hands!

Since lines on your hands can also be genetically driven (if many others in your family tend to have similar lines), it could mean you were sent back with your family group to work out some group karma; in other words, maybe you're all working out old issues, breaking old patterns, and moving forward to a happier, healthier family life.

FACT

In a past-life palm reading, both hands can be read the same way as in a regular reading. Your dominant hand represents what you actually accomplished in life, and your other hand represents what your potential for life really was. If most of your lines are very faint, you still have quite a bit to accomplish in this life!

Palmistry for Personal Growth

One of the main reasons to read palms for spiritual patterns or belief systems is to use this information as an informative key in determining an individual's potential for personal growth. If a person has strong convictions and beliefs, he or she is more likely to survive any tumultuous situations that could be made evident by other lines on the hands.

The important thing when looking at less favorable lines of the hand is to think not in terms of life's challenges, but in terms of the opportunities they present for positive change and growth. Working through the difficulties and challenges in life is how we eventually reach our life's fullest potential.

Those who have the faintest lines on their hands, particularly with respect to those closest to Jupiter, have the most opportunity for spiritual and emotional growth through all of their life's lessons. They also tend to have the smoothest ride on the road to spiritual enlightenment, because their lines are not deeply set. On the other hand, those with deeper lines can be said to have already achieved the height of their personal awareness—a blissful state of "nirvana," the highest level of peace and oneness with all they believe.

Spirit Lines and Your Life's Work

Now that you've examined the lines, mounts, and patterns on your hands, looking for clues to the great mysteries of your life, you can take your reading a step further with a look at how far your spirituality is likely to take you in this life. For instance, if you have the loop of empathy, combined with simian lines and a dominant Jupiter mount, you are predestined for success as a spiritual leader in whatever belief system you choose to accept.

Look at your Jupiter mount: Does it show that you believe in miracles? If it is well developed, you are more likely to ask for spiritual assistance or guidance in all aspects of your life. But remember that you are the one who is ultimately responsible for making personal changes to affect the lines on your hands.

Hospice workers and those in the healthcare profession often have the spatulate-shaped "Healer's Hand"; the more alternative healers tend to have the psychic or pointed hands with lots of empathy loops or simian lines. The great philanthropists typically have wide, open hands with bent-back thumbs, and their lines and empathy loops tend to be deeper than others.

Of course, just because you have convincingly deep lines of spirit does not necessarily mean you must heed the spiritual call that seems to appear on your palm—as with anything else in life, you are given free will so that you can make whatever choice makes the most sense to you.

You could choose to work in human resources management, offering your spiritual gift to be a "guide" to those in the workplace. Or you could decide to share your spiritual gifts by reading to the blind, or by volunteering at a local soup kitchen on weekends. Ⓔ

Chapter 19

Reading for Others

One of the most fun things you can do is read palms for your family, friends, and acquaintances. Or—who knows—you might even become a professional palm reader! Palmistry is an enormously rewarding practice. When you read someone else's palm, you're not only connecting with them, you're also connecting with a vast knowledge base derived from thousands of years of tradition.

Your Role as a Reader

When you sit down to read someone else's palms, their future is literally in your hands. In less than one hour, you will play many roles in this person's life—from counselor and spiritual advisor to mentor and coach. You will identify many unique qualities, challenges, and opportunities, but you may also help to clarify a person's sacred path in life.

As a counselor and spiritual advisor, you will take a close look at the lines on people's hands to determine how they've handled the joys, trials, and tribulations of life—and their tendencies for handling them in the future. You'll get an up-close-and-personal look at their inner selves; you'll be their trusted friend and confidant. You'll hear about the challenges they faced when young, and what their main concerns are at this point in their lives.

ALERT!

The information you learn during a palm reading should be kept strictly confidential! Confidentiality between reader and client is of the utmost importance and a tremendous responsibility—one that you must take very seriously if you want to be a professional palm reader.

Answers to Life's Bigger Questions

When clients consult you for a palm reading, they most likely want to know the answers to life's bigger questions, such as "Why am I here—what is my purpose?" and "When will I find my life partner?" But your role may well extend beyond mere answers to the perennial questions of life. You may also find yourself encouraging them to overcome their hindering tendencies and challenges as presented in the lines on their hands. In this sense, you will be more of a coach or mentor, instilling in them the concept that they indeed are masters of their own fate and have a choice in their behaviors or circumstances. You can be an inspiring voice—encouraging them to succeed in life!

How much should I charge?
Professional palm readers typically charge anywhere from $15 for a fifteen-minute reading to $100 for an hour-long reading. Try doing your first few readings for free in order to start building a clientele.

Preparing for a Reading

How do you prepare yourself to open your mind and heart to helping another person? You begin by clearing your mind of any preconceptions—and then clear the space in your environment. Find a quiet, designated space for doing private readings. Many palm readers have small tables covered with a soft velvet tablecloth.

There are lots of things you might have on the table. Helpful tools for a palm reading include the following:

- A notebook or a tape recorder to keep a record of the reading for your client
- A magnifying glass (for those fine, hard-to-read lines)
- Some crystals (if they help you focus)
- Incense (preferably patchouli or lavender, which are believed to offer protection)
- A few candles (for effect)
- Some soft, simple music (Chinese flute music or anything in the New Age category will work just fine)
- A timer with a soft alarm sound so that your client will gently be reminded when their time is up (otherwise, most readings do run overtime)
- A good palmistry reference book, especially if you're still a beginning reader

Once you get more used to doing readings, you may find lots of other objects to add to your list. Many palm readers have portable reading tables so they can offer readings at festivals, flea markets, and other public places. If you decide to go public with your palm reading, be sure to secure the proper business licenses so that you don't violate any of your local tax laws. You wouldn't want anyone to shut down your booth!

Many professional palm readers use a compass and ruler in order to measure proportions and lines of the hands. These can be particularly useful when trying to determine actual time lines for specific life events.

Your most important tool, however, is yourself. Make sure you are in a happy, healthy state of mind, body, and spirit. If you're feeling off-kilter, your reading may be affected by it, and you do want happy clients who refer others to you for additional business—not dissatisfied customers who tell others your reading was not up to par. If you're going to do this professionally, you must have this kind of sensitivity toward your clients.

Setting the Tone

Most professional palm readers are experts at setting the proper tone for doing a reading. The lights are dim, there are plenty of candles and incense, and the music perfectly sets the mood for concentration. But what else do they do to prepare for giving the highest-quality reading they can muster?

Some readers begin with a meditation or prayer. When you begin with a prayer, you are immediately connecting to a higher power to help you offer the best insights and information for your client. You are allowing the positive energy of the universe to flow from your heart and hands into the client's—ensuring a reading that will best serve the client's interests, needs, and desires.

Turn off the phone and remove anything that will interfere with your concentration. Even before the client appears, you can start with some deep breathing exercises to facilitate clear thinking and a peaceful demeanor. As you inhale and exhale deeply, begin your prayer: "O Loving Spirit, let your wisdom pour into my hands so that it may also fill the hands of my clients. Help me to help them find their way through this earthly life—to instill in them the knowledge that they always have choices, and that here today we look to the plan in their hands as only a guide or aid along the way."

Taking Their Hands into Yours

When the client is with you and you've already completed the initial assessment, take her hands in yours and hold them for a brief moment. Free your mind, close your eyes, and allow yourself to feel the impressions of her hands in yours. What are your feelings about these hands? Where have they been, and where are they going?

Many professional palm readers combine methods of spiritual readings for their clients. They might begin with a quick look at the three major lines, then do a tarot card reading or crystal reading to confirm what they are picking up psychically. It's okay to combine methods, provided you know enough about each to make the information valuable to your client.

Allow your mind to record its own impressions in this "energy reading" of your client's hands. The more practice you get using this psychic version of palm reading, the better a reader you'll become with time. You'll be amazed at how much information you can pick up about a person just from touching her hands—without even looking at the major lines yet!

Letting the Story Unfold

When you are reading the palms of another person, you might notice that the lines, shapes, and textures of the hand seem to tell stories within stories. Many experienced readers will tell you that they only read hands as a starting point in piecing together the story of a person's life. Over time, as you gain more experience reading hands, you'll find too that palm reading is a lot like painting a picture—you start with some quick sketches, then fill in the lines with some colors or shading and, before you know it, the painting seems to finish itself. Though it might be vastly different from your original inspiration, the finished product is a work of art and belongs to only you.

So it is with the intuitive art of palm reading. You are helping another person to create or even recreate their life story—in the flesh of their palm. Learn to listen to your intuition as closely as your intellect when you are doing a palm reading for yourself or others. Use common sense, especially when looking at the palm's color and texture for signs of good health. For instance, it's obvious that a scaly white hand with rough texture isn't as vibrant and healthy as a smooth, pinkish one.

Reading Between Lines

You don't really need a book on palmistry to tell you that—but you do need a book like this one in order to decipher the fine lines between your head and your heart. Once you learn everything you can, your own techniques and practices will become more apparent and you'll find that it becomes much easier to read palms using a combination of time-tested skill and your own intuitive abilities. Celebrate what you can bring to this incredible, ancient art!

Handling Expectations

When someone comes to you for a palm reading, she is putting her faith in your hands. You need to be honest, reassuring, and sensitive to her needs—but you don't need to be a doormat for her. Set your boundaries early on regarding length and price of the reading, perhaps even at the appointment stage. Let her know what your policies or expectations are of her as a client.

A palm reading is very much a two-way street. Simply put, if your clients are expecting honesty and sincerity from you, they should also be willing to extend these courtesies to you as their reader and advisor. Under no circumstances are you obligated to read for everyone—if you don't feel safe in a certain situation, you don't need to participate in it.

Decide ahead of time what you're comfortable with, and be sure to include such information in your promotional material such as a brochure or Web site.

FACT

Beginner palm readers often use palm printing as a practice tool so that they can take their time doing a reading without the added pressure of having to "perform" for a person. Any practice you can get, whether from ink-prints or photocopies of a hand, will help you develop your palm-reading abilities.

Dealing with the Needy

One of the most common things that can happen to you as a palm reader is that you could wind up with an extremely needy person—someone who relentlessly asks you to read for them, and seeks guidance in areas where perhaps it would be best for the situation to be permitted to unfold on its own. With people like this, it's best to say that it is not a good idea to do too many readings too close together—that readings should, in fact, be at least a few months apart, since they can cover about a six-month to one-year period. Then, when they do call you again for another reading, ask them to focus on one or two things they would like to know, rather than a complete laundry list of every issue that's on their mind at the moment. By keeping them focused and their readings well timed, you'll be able to offer the best reading value—while preserving your own sanity and need for space!

Doing a Simple Reading

To begin the actual reading, take a few moments to look at the client's hands and how she holds them. It's always a good idea to do this in order to make some initial assessments. Look at the size, shape, and condition of the hands. How does she hold them—close to her body (suggesting shyness or introversion) or eagerly open in front of you (suggesting that this is an open, secure person who is unafraid of learning more about herself). This informal preliminary examination can really enhance the reading of the lines later on.

A good time to look at the client's hands is when you ask her to write her name, date of birth, and what it is that she would like to learn on a piece of paper before the reading begins. This will keep the client occupied—and not self-conscious—as she might otherwise be if she knew you were staring at her hands.

An Overview of the Lines

Once you've conducted your initial visual assessment of the hands, it's time to do the overview reading of the lines. Start with the three major lines, in whatever order most appeals to you. Most readers begin with the head and life lines, since they begin in the childhood area of the hand's time line. When looking at these lines, you can determine what kind of childhood the client had (for example, you can check to see whether she has lots of chains, indicating a tough childhood; or simple, straightforward lines, which represent a smooth and happy childhood). Then, you can move on to the heart line.

Remember to read both hands to compare the person's potential in life (secondary hand) with their actual life path (the hand they write with and use most). This way, you can best offer insight into how well the person is living up to their potential.

What you're looking for in these three major lines, at least for a quick overview type of reading, is how deep the lines are, whether there are any breaks or special markings, and the length or timing of specific life events (see Chapter 11 for a review of timing). For instance, you might see that the life line breaks off and then another part of the line continues on to the wrist bracelets or rascettes. This means that the client may make a major change in her life at a later stage—for instance, she might decide to sell everything and cruise around the world on a sailboat. Or maybe it's a more simple and practical change, such as moving to a warmer climate after retirement. The other lines, and your own psychic impressions, will help you figure out exactly what kind of shift may be in the client's future.

Sum up the three major lines and what they show at the close of your overview reading. Always keep things on a positive note, and end with a blessing for the client, even if it's as simple as "Go in peace."

The quick overview reading can be fun, but reading only the three main lines in fifteen minutes doesn't offer the most complete reading. Be sure to remind your subject that there are many other lines that provide more detail. Of course, there should be an extra charge for a longer, more detailed palm reading.

An In-Depth Hand Analysis

Once you become a more experienced reader, you'll come to notice that there are several very typical questions that clients ask:

- What is my personality like?
- Am I going to succeed in my business or career?
- Will I be married soon?
- How many children will I have?
- What are my prospects for a long life?
- Will I be wealthy?
- When will I be able to retire?
- Will I be famous or well known?
- Do you see any warning signs on my hands?

Most of these questions can be answered in the quick overview reading, but some may require a more in-depth reading of both hands. Get out your magnifying glass and start making some detailed notes for the more difficult questions posed by your clients—and don't be afraid to say, "I'm not sure," if the lines are hard to read or if you are simply not certain what you're seeing. Admitting you don't know can actually build a client's confidence level in your abilities as a reader; there's nothing more damaging to a client than misrepresentation. Remember, they are vulnerable and deserve to know the truth about all aspects of their readings.

Take Your Time

An in-depth reading requires at least thirty minutes, but preferably one hour of your time. The reason for this is that you are going to look at not only the three major lines, but also the mounts of the fingers and palm, the overall skin condition and tone, secondary lines and patterns, and other important features—basically, everything we've covered in this book!

ALERT!

> Try to stay objective and emotionally detached as you read someone else's hands. Weigh each word carefully—there are plenty of things you might see in the hands that might seem on first reading to be negative but which later turn out to be surmountable.

Some readers ask their clients to provide a photocopy of their hands ahead of time so that they can do a preliminary assessment prior to the in-depth, in-person reading. That's fine, but be sure to write notes so that you don't spend your in-person time going over things that you've already covered. You can quickly go over the notes from the photocopies, then look at the actual hands to begin the in-depth reading.

Dealing with Major Issues and Concerns

In the in-depth reading, more than likely you will be dealing with lots of major issues, concerns, and questions from your client. While it's perfectly fine to ask the client to focus on one or two main questions at the beginning of the reading, you'll find that there's time to go into greater detail, discussing hopes, dreams, and future possibilities.

You can begin with the basic personality assessment, followed by an initial hand assessment and overview, and then veer off into as many different issues and directions as your time will allow. At the end of it all, don't forget to ask your client if she feels satisfied with the reading, and whether all questions have been answered. You'll want her to leave feeling like she has a better sense of herself, with a more confident outlook regarding her future.

When your reading is finished and your client leaves, you should do a "space cleansing" and reclaim your own energy, as much was likely expended in the reading itself. The best way to reclaim energy is to burn some lavender incense and take a relaxing sea salt luxury bath. You've earned it!

Charging for Your Services

Regarding the practice of charging your clients for readings: Yes, you *should* charge for your time—and always ask for your money upfront, removing it from the table during the reading. Psychologically speaking, you don't want your client always looking at the money, wondering whether they're getting their money's worth during the reading. You want (and need) their full attention at all times during the reading to make it really meaningful and to be sure your client understands everything you're saying to them about their palm reading. Keep them focused on the service at hand, so to speak!

Do I need a license to practice palmistry?
No, but if you want to make your living from it, you might want to consider joining the Better Business Bureau to protect your reputation. There are lots of charlatans out there, and you'll want to quickly set yourself apart from them.

Chapter 20

Palmistry and Other Spiritual Arts

Palmistry is a fascinating area of divination. You can rely on it as it stands, or you can combine it with other awareness and perception arts, which share the idea that there is a link between the individual person and the entirety of creation, and which regard each individual as a microcosm (a smaller model) of the macrocosm (the universe at large). Your hand might be a map of your persona, but it is also a way to chart the cosmos.

Combining Intuitive Arts

When you are reading palms, you may find that you would like to rely on some of the other esoteric or intuitive arts such as astrology, crystals, or tarot. If you are a well-developed psychic practitioner whose experience includes these other forms of divination, feel free to let your intuition guide you in combining your readings to give your subjects a deeper look inside themselves.

If, on the other hand, you are not as experienced in calling in other intuitive energies in combination with a palm reading, make sure you read this chapter for an introduction to reflexology, astrology, psychic reading, Vedic palmistry, the Chakras, and *I Ching*. These ancient arts support and enhance each other in the study of advanced palmistry.

The Art of Reflexology

Reflexology is related to acupuncture and is widely practiced in China. Both systems are based on the idea that energy, or *chi*, circulates along pathways in the body. These pathways connect all of the internal parts of the body—the organs and glands—and when the energy in these pathways is blocked, the result is discomfort and even disease.

However, it is possible to unblock the paths and get the energy moving again. In acupuncture, you can halt or stimulate the body's energy by inserting fine needles into the most appropriate of the 800 nodes. In reflexology, the same is achieved through massage or another form of stimulation of these nodes.

Connection to Palmistry

Many of the nodes recognized by reflexology and acupuncture are located on the hands and the feet, so a hand reading and a reflexology session have a great deal in common. In a reading, the palmist feels the hand, exploring the mounts and hollows, in a process very similar to reflexology.

While you are examining the lines, mounts, and fingers of your subject, you can also massage the palms, the areas between the tendons, the webs of the fingers, working from the wrist to the fingertips to enhance blood flow. You can also gently bend and stretch the fingers, thumb, and wrists forward and back after the session. Finish with a gentle pressing and rubbing all over the hand, and your clients will be standing in line for your readings.

Astrology: Reading the Stars

Palmistry and astrology have much in common, as they are both organized systems by which people can come to a better understanding of their strengths and weaknesses, surroundings and influences, the past and the future. A person's palm is very similar to a birth chart, as both are indications of his character, intelligence, emotional life, abilities, environment, relationships, and future possibilities.

The two systems also share a great deal of the same terminology, so the palmist already has a good head start when exploring astrology. For instance, both systems use the names of the sun, moon, and planets, which palmistry applies to the fingers and mounts of the hands.

Planetary Fingers

Each of the four fingers—named after sun (Apollo) and the planets Mercury, Jupiter, and Saturn—are subdivided into three phalanges. Four fingers multiplied by three phalanges give you twelve—one phalange for each of the twelve signs of the zodiac. How these are assigned is very interesting, as it does not conform to either the course of the year or the layout of the hand. Instead, the phalanges serve to describe and buoy the strengths of each individual finger:

- **The Jupiter finger:** The area of justice. The three phalanges, starting from the finger tip and going down to the base, are Aries the Ram, which represents leadership and spiritual power; Taurus the Bull, which represents ambition and perseverance; and Gemini the Twins, which represents financial acuity and influence. All of these signs are true representatives of the kingly and dominating Jupiter finger.

- **The Apollo finger:** The sun finger's phalanges include Cancer the Crab (the top phalange), which is ruled by the moon and represents creativity and originality; Leo the Lion, which indicates expressiveness and talent and augments Cancer; and Virgo, the analytical sign that shows the critical abilities needed in art. Together, these three signs signify Apollo's artistic and aesthetic sense wonderfully.
- **The Mercury finger:** This finger's three phalanges are, beginning with the top one, Libra the Scales, a sign of balance, diplomacy, openness, and communication; Scorpio the Scorpion, which describes personal communication and truthfulness; and Sagittarius the Archer, which stands for honesty, forthrightness, feeling, and spirit. All three typify the communicative Mercury.
- **The Saturn finger:** This finger, which ends the zodiac year, includes Capricorn the Goat, a sign of morality and orthodoxy; Aquarius the Water Bearer, a phalange that represents selflessness and the quest for knowledge; and Pisces the Fish, which stands for conformity and decorum. All of these support the saturnine elements of structure, discipline, and study.

ESSENTIAL

The palm and finger mounts also have astrological names, so the astrological palmist can gain even more information from them. The mount of Venus, for example, represents the second planet as well as the goddess of beauty and love, and like the mount she shows the qualities of physical attractiveness, liveliness, and emotion.

You can look at each one of the phalanges and its markings in order to get some information about a particular aspect of your life or personality. Here is what you may find:

- **Vertical lines:** Flowing energy, a positive aspect
- **Horizontal lines:** Blocked energy—a retrograde, or backward-moving, aspect
- **Grilles:** Confused and diffused energy, a neutral or negative aspect

- **Crosses:** Diverted energy, a negative aspect
- **Stars:** An abundance of energy, which may be a positive or a negative aspect
- **Clear areas:** Potential energy, a positive aspect

The moon is also seen in the hand in the mount of Luna, an area that controls the subconscious, spirituality and intuition, with all the moon's mystery and intangible changeability.

Other Planetary Influences

The other planets can be found in the hand as well. The positive and negative Mars mounts, on either side of the hand, show the aggressive and active elements of the warrior god and fifth planet, along with his courage, strength, and endurance. The mount of Neptune, the god of the ocean and eighth planet, lies between the Venus and Luna mounts at the point where the conscious and unconscious meet, and this god of the deep shows the harmony that essentially lies between them. The mount of Uranus (on the thumb side of the wrist) tells of the attributes of the god of the sky, who is the father of Saturn and the grandfather of Jupiter, as well as the namesake of the seventh planet. Finally, the ninth planet, and the god of the underworld, Pluto, is seen in the hand on the mount that lies near the wrist on the side away from the thumb. They live on the cusp between the mind and the biological body.

FACT

There are currently more than 10,000 palm readers in the United States alone—and probably several more thousand in countries as diverse as India, China, and Greece.

Conducting Psychic Readings

Just as people are now using mutually supportive exercises such as yoga and medication to improve their quality of life, many psychic readers use the palm as a launch pad to a deeper, more holistic reading. Self-awareness leads to fulfillment as you discover your own unique psyche and reach a higher level of understanding, so you can balance your mind, body, and spirit—the psychological, physical, and spiritual parts of life.

Interpreting the Quadrants

One way to approach this is to look at the hand as having four quadrants. In your mind, divide your hand in half vertically, to separate the thumb side (which represents the conscious self) and the percussion side (the unconscious self). Then, divide your palm in half horizontally; the upper portion represents intellectual aspects and the lower portion your feelings and emotional life.

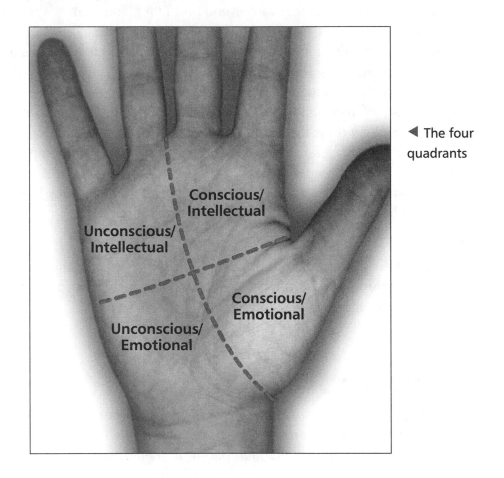

◀ The four quadrants

1. The conscious/intellectual quadrant includes the Jupiter and Saturn fingers and mounts. Look to this quadrant to learn more about your physical life, daily doings, possessions, and intellectual matters.
2. The conscious/emotional quadrant includes the Luna mount and thumbs and shows such areas as your sexuality, passion, ability to love, recklessness, response to art, and sense of identity.
3. The unconscious/intellectual quadrant includes the Apollo and Mercury fingers and mounts; it shows the mental aspects of life that sustain you from within, such as your ability with art, science, and communication.
4. The unconscious/emotional quadrant includes the Luna mount and shows your pleasure centers, spiritual areas, intuition, psychic ability, self-involvement, and playfulness.

To assess a person, look at the markings in each quadrant, and interpret them using the explanations of markings provided in the previous section on astrology. If you have an abundance of lines in a certain quadrant, that is an indication of where your psychic energy is concentrated.

Psychic Hand Reading

The study of palmistry can help the psychic interpret the course of a life. As you progress along the life line, you begin at the edge of the hand, near the Jupiter finger. This represents your entry into the outside world, the external domain ruled by Jupiter, when you begin to learn the culture you are born into. You then pass into the domain of Saturn on the life line, an area guided by Saturn's thirst for knowledge and study and a time when education and schooling predominate.

FACT

The Chinese, Vedic Indian, ancient Greek, and Egyptian cultures all practiced palmistry as a way of studying the person and helping him understand more about himself and his future, as well as his relationship to others and to the world at large.

Then you reach maturity in the realm of Apollo, a time when you go into the world and use your creativity to make an independent life. Finally, in the last part of the maturation process, you enter the realm of Mercury on the life line, when you begin to establish a career and business skills needed to make a living. At this time, you are about halfway along the life line, and it swerves around the Venus mount, as you gain familial and other relationships and new interests, with your life growing to its close.

Vedic Palmistry

The sacred Hindu scriptures are called the Vedas, the storehouse of all knowledge, and they are the oldest literature in India, more than 5,000 years old. There are four major books and six appendices called the *sadvedangas,* the limbs of the Vedas, which explain how to read and use the scriptures. One of the Vedas, the *jyotisa* (light from God), concerns astronomy and astrology, which also includes tips on reading the body. Also known as the eye of the Vedas, so called because it is concerned with time cycles, it lets us see through time so we can understand the workings of nature.

In the Vedic system, astrology is a dictionary created by Lord Krishna so we can read the signs and understand the language of time by using the horoscope, or birth chart, and the zodiac, or sky clock. The planets do not have the power to direct fate, but they do describe and measure it.

The study of the parts of the body—including the mouth, ears, legs, feet, and hands—is a branch of astronomy, and the study of the hands is called *Hasta Samudrika Shastra,* which translates as "the ocean of knowledge concerning signs and symbols of the hand." Thus, palmistry and astrology are very intimately related.

Nine Heavenly Bodies

In Vedic astrology, there are nine planets, or heavenly bodies, but they differ somewhat from those of the West:

1. *The sun:* Concerns God, the life force, the masculine principal, command, renown, self-esteem, and the external, that which we show to the world.

2. *The moon:* Concerns the female principal, emotional life, the mind, intuition, and our true internal nature.
3. *Mercury:* Concerns communication, education, and thought.
4. *Venus:* Concerns love, sex, the arts, creativity, food, pleasure, and money.
5. *Mars:* Concerns conflict, force, activity, endurance, and determination.
6. *Jupiter:* Concerns marriage and children, religion, knowledge, and fortune.
7. *Saturn:* Concerns discipline, limitation, truth, and duty.

So far, Vedic astrology is much like that of the West, but there are two additions. Instead of the outer planets, the Vedic system includes two lunar modes:

8. **Rahu:** The lunar north mode, concerning materialism, instability, and the unconventional and unorthodox.
9. **Ketu:** The lunar south mode, concerning antimaterialism, social order, and the spiritual life and orthodoxy.

FACT

According to Vedic palmistry, the fate line shows the expression of the unconscious thoughts found in your major lines and the structure you have brought to your life.

The Three Gunas

The Vedic practitioner looks at the same elements as his Western counterpart when doing a palm reading, examining the three *gunas,* or levels of awareness. To him, the major lines show your subconscious, the positive and negative patterns of thought that direct how you live, think, and feel without a planned response, as seen in the life, head, and heart lines, just as it is in the West.

The minor lines show your consciousness, what you are actually aware of regarding your own life and destiny. Again, this is very similar to the West's interpretation.

Interpreting the Mounts

The mounts show your superconscious, the consciousness as it is applied in the world, or how you have faced your challenges and what you have accomplished in the areas controlled by each mount. These, too, are similar to Western tradition and found in the same places, and they basically follow the previous list that describes the planets in astrology. In addition to the other planet mounts, the mount of Rahu, which takes the place of the plain of Mars, stands for your current environment, while Ketu, which is found where the West places the mount of Neptune, is the past, your karmic inheritance, and how you feel about it.

Palmistry and the Chakras

A *chakra,* a Sanskrit word for "moving wheel," is an energy field in our physical being that concentrates the energy of the universe that keeps us alive. There are seven major chakras and many minor ones, and they are centered in our bodies along the spine.

The chakras serve to channel the energy, or life force, to the relevant parts of the body. Various chakras control our reason, emotion, and will, which must be in balance for us to function well. However, these chakras can be blocked through fear, pain, or stress, disturbing the balance of energy of the body.

The seven major chakras are seen from the base of the spine upward, in ascending order of spiritual progress:

1. *Muladhara:* This chakra, ruled by Saturn, is the root at the base of the spine. It represents the material world, your job and skills, and the need for basic physical survival.
2. *Svadisthana:* This chakra, ruled by Jupiter, is located near the belly button. It represents sexuality, creativity, the appetites, and excess.
3. *Manipura:* This chakra, ruled by Mars, lies at the solar plexus. It represents power, strength, aggression, and control.
4. *Anahatha:* Ruled by Venus, this chakra lies at the heart. It represents love, compassion, beauty, and harmony.

5. *Vishudda:* Located at the throat, this chakra represents creativity, speech, and communications. It is ruled by Mercury.
6. *Anja:* Ruled by the moon, this chakra is located at the brow and represents inner thought, vision, dreams, and the third eye.
7. *Sehasara:* Ruled by the sun, the crown chakra is at the top of the head. It represents the consciousness of god, transcendence beyond self.

The Chakras and Duality

One approach to the chakras is to interpret them astrologically. By assigning the chakras a duality, either a masculine and feminine principal, an inner-seeking or outward-seeking identity, or a day and night persona, the lower six chakras can be used to represent the signs of the zodiac, with the crown chakra ruling all. Today, some practitioners are creating horoscopes using this system.

However, because this book concentrates on palmistry, it is more important to explain how the chakras relate to the hand and how it is then interpreted. It's important for you to remember that the chakras represent nodes in which the energy flow is concentrated and directed to the parts of the body from the universe. There are several minor chakras in addition to the major ones described so far, and these are places where energy, called *chi* in other systems, can be unblocked. It's very reminiscent of how reflexology and acupuncture are used to unblock energy and lead to healing.

The study of the hand can also guide you in using your talents and abilities and can help you to understand those that still lie untapped within you so you can bring them forward to be used in the outside world.

The palms are such a place, as they are rife with energy nodes, being "out there" in the world. They, along with the fingertips, receive energy and information from the universe and transmit it to others, using it to understand and to heal.

Opening the Flow of Energy

Many believe that the chakras of the hand can be deliberately opened to allow the flow of energy to increase and be directed. The chakra of the right hand is related to playfulness and joy, and it also lets us find our way when we are confused or feel lost, so it kindles our spirit of adventure. Thus, it represents homecoming and belonging, whether to an earthly or a spiritual home. Blocked energy in the right palm can lead to immaturity and childishness or to fear of independence, new experiences, and growth.

Western civilization is undergoing a radical change, where the rational and scientific are giving way to a better understanding of what Eastern practices have to offer, with their emphasis on inner development, respect for energy fields within and without, and our links to the universe and nature.

In the left hand, the chakra energy controls our view of the afterlife, and blockage can make us fearful of death, another kind of adventure. The left hand records the joy we have felt in the past and our sense of accomplishment in our deeds, the deeds that will go with us into the afterlife. The left hand is also a place where our inner thoughts are made manifest in our actions, so blockage of this chakra can keep us from effective work.

Introduction to *I Ching*

The Chinese and Occidental systems of palmistry do have many similarities, but it may take some time and study of both systems in order to find them. The Chinese system goes beyond the palm to pay greater attention to the wrists and the thumb, as well as the minor lines, which can sometimes be read as ideograms.

The Chinese method of palmistry uses the *I Ching*, which has the same regard for the flow of energy, or *chi*, as does *feng shui*, the art of placement. These two systems also share a reliance on geographical direction, the major elements, and the seasons, and see these elements as dualities, leading to a system of palmistry that is beautiful to talk about and ponder on.

> In China, palm reading is far more highly regarded than it is in the West, and palmists are consulted both in daily life and before important events and undertakings.

The *I Ching* says that there are eight mounts on the hand, at each of the cardinal directions (north, east, south, and west) and the points between them (northeast, southeast, southwest, northwest).

A Handy Octagon

To begin to understand Chinese palmistry, think of the palm as an octagon, with the south at the top by the fingers (this is counterintuitive to our Northern hemisphere maps if you are reading your own palm, but sensible if reading another's); the north at the bottom; the east on the side of the thumb; and the west on the percussion side. These mounts also represent the circle of the year and the course of the day.

1. *Southeast:* Located where our Jupiter mount would be, this mount represents versatility, peacefulness, and gentle effectiveness. It is the mount of early summer and the middle of the morning.
2. *South:* Located at the Saturn mount, it represents intelligence, insight, grace, and refinement. The timing for this mount is noontime and midsummer, when the sun is at its height.
3. *Southwest:* This mount, which covers Apollo and Mercury mounts, shows the ability to receive, with the idea of spaciousness and passiveness. It is the mount of early fall, when crops are ripened, and of the night.
4. *West:* Located at the Lower Mars mount, this area represents fullness, completion, satiation, and gratification; the timing for this mount is late fall, or dusk, and it represents the setting sun in the west.
5. *Northwest:* Located on the mount of Luna, this mount represents

creativity, endurance, and force; it spans the early winter and is the mount of daytime.

6. *North:* Covering the mount of Neptune (on the lower part of the hand), this is the area of hardship, fear, and possible peril. It represents the hard and cold middle of winter, as well as midnight.

7. *Northeast:* Located at the mount of Venus, this area represents the time of waiting, restfulness, calmness, and patience; the timing of the northeast is the late winter, when we wait for spring's arrival, and the time of dawn, as day is about to commence.

8. *East:* The upper Mars area is a place of activity, awakening, and energy. In the circle of the year that is superimposed on the palm in these mounts, it represents the beginning of the year, spring, as well as the early morning, as the sun is about to rise in the east.

Notice that although the seasons follow a complete circle around the mounts, the times of day vary a little. In traditional Chinese palmistry, the mounts are all family members, with the father, representing northeast, the daytime, and the mother, the southeast, the nighttime. If you take these away, the children mounts do go in order.

Palmistry and You

The hands and fingers are very meaningful organs. We use them to work, to pray, to bless, to speak, to create. They serve as intermediaries between ourselves and the world and they make us uniquely human.

The study of the hand, its lines, mounts, and shapes is a good way to learn more about yourself and your role in the cosmos. Just as your hand is unique and specific to you as an individual, so too are you a unique individual in the world, with unique talents, skills, and characteristics. Using what you learn from the study of the hand, you can take it upon yourself to expand both your outer and inner lives, making sure that the world your create for yourself is the best one for you. Ⓔ

Appendices

Appendix A

Glossary

Appendix B

Additional Resources

Glossary

air hand: The air hand features a round-shaped palm with long, slender fingers; it is known as the artistic hand.

Apollo finger: The third (or ring) finger. In palmistry, this finger represents creative spirit and a sense of inner balance.

Apollo line: This line ends on the mount just below the Apollo finger and shows the degree of inner satisfaction through creativity.

Apollo mount: A mount or raised muscular area under the third or Apollo finger. This mount is said to predict the potential for fame and personal wealth through creativity.

arch: Representing the more practical and material nature of the individual, arches are small, raised line patterns that occur on fingerprints. They can be either subtle or quite pronounced.

bar: A short line (or series of lines) that appears to cut through a major line, symbolically creating an obstacle for the individual in a particular area of his or her life.

bow of intuition: One of the many secondary patterns that can occur on the percussion just beneath the Mercury or fourth finger. This marking is quite apparent on psychics and other highly intuitive people.

bracelets: Also known as "rascettes," these are the lines located across the wrists. According to Eastern palmistry, having three or more rascettes indicates a long life.

break: Any interruption in the flow or direction of lines, indicating change that happens against our will.

chain: A series of links or islands that appear in patterns on the palm, usually along one of the three major lines.

chirognomy: The study of inherited hand characteristics, including shape, texture, movement, and more.

chirology: The more traditional name for the total combined study of chirognomy and chiromancy.

chiromancy: The study of the lines of the palms. For many years, this was the way palms were read with the reader only looking at the lines and not taking shape, size, and consistency of the hand into account.

conical shape: The shape of the hand that is best seen when the fingers are all held together and the hand seems to be cone-shaped.

cross: Crosses are obstacle lines that occur anywhere on the palm or fingertips; their criss-crossed patterns signify opposition.

curved percussion: When the palm appears to have a noticeably curved or bowlike outer edge.

dermatoglyphics: The study of skin ridge patterns occurring on the palms and fingertips.

dermatitis: A condition of the skin that causes dry, cracked texture and can affect lines on the hand.

destiny line: See **fate line.**

dominant hand: The hand you use most often for writing, eating, and performing tactile actions.

earth hand: A square hand with small, short fingers, it represents a practical, down-to-earth nature.

fate line: The major line that spans the vertical length of the palm, indicating your destined path in life. It can also pertain to career.

fire hand: Rectangular hand with short, spatulate-shaped fingers that represents an active, energetic personality.

Girdle of Venus: A special marking that can occur between the Saturn and Apollo fingers. Anxious, hypersensitive people tend to have this mark.

grille: Also known in palmistry as anxiety marks, these mixed line patterns (consisting of both horizontal and vertical lines in a gridlike pattern) are quite common.

head line: One of the three major lines in palm reading, this line extends horizontally under the four finger mounts and represents a person's intellectual abilities.

heart line: Located under the head line, this major line speaks to the individual's emotional state and sense of giving.

island: When a line splits in one place but then reconnects nearby, this is known as an island on the palm. Islands typically mean that the individual suffers from a marked lack of energy or vitality.

Jupiter finger: The first finger, pertaining to leadership ability and business sense.

Jupiter mount: Located just beneath the Jupiter or first finger, this mount represents the person's sense of inner strength and ownership.

life line: This major line curves near the thumb, downward toward the wrist. It signifies a person's health, vitality, and quality of life.

loop: Circular patterns that can be found either on the palms or on fingerprints.

Lower Mars mount: Found just above the Luna or moon mount, this mount shows honesty, integrity, and general endurance.

luna mount: The mount or raised muscular area on the outer palm of the hand that deals with matters of imagination, intuition, and creativity.

major lines: The three primary lines of the hand, including the head, heart, and life lines; can also include the fate line.

Mars line: This line is found along the life line and is considered to be protective in nature.

Mercury finger: The fourth or little finger representing communication in the broad sense and temper in a limited sense.

Mercury line: One of the secondary lines occurring on the palm; indicates whether the individual has strong business skill or good health.

Mercury mount: The mount or fleshy pad located just underneath the fourth or Mercury finger that deals with health, commerce, and travel.

mixed hand: A rare hand type that incorporates many different shapes and characteristics that defy easy categorization.

moon: A crescent-shaped marking, usually white, on the surface of the fingernail.

Neptune mount: This mount, rarely mentioned in palmistry, is located between the Luna or moon mount and the Venus mount. A thickly padded Neptune mount indicates charisma.

palmar ridges: The raised portions of the palm and their corresponding patterns.

palmistry: The ancient intuitive art of studying the hands to determine personality, health, and potential in life.

passive hand: The hand you use less often for major tasks; the opposite of the dominant hand.

patterns: Designs that occur naturally on the surface of the fingertips and palms.

Peacock's Eye: A whorl pattern that is encircled or contained within a loop pattern on the fingertips or palm. This is a protective sign, but often belongs to those with physical disabilities.

percussion: The outer edge of the hand, away from the thumb side of the hand. The shape of your percussion demonstrates whether you have a creative or practical personality.

phalanges: The individual sections of each finger, from joint to joint.

plain of Mars: The valley of the palm, surrounded by all of the raised mounts.

pointed hand: The shape that forms a point when the fingers are held together and the hand is examined in a flat, openhanded position. Pointed hands are often called psychic hands, since many intuitive types have this hand shape.

rascettes: The bracelets or lines of the wrist.

Ring of Apollo: This rather uncommon, curved line wraps around the Apollo finger near the mount of Apollo and denotes impaired creativity.

Ring of Saturn: Often called the pessimist's mark, this ringlike line can be located just under the Saturn finger (above the Saturn mount).

Ring of Solomon: Just as the biblical leader Solomon was known for his wisdom, so it is with those whose hands sport a ringlike line around their Jupiter finger.

Saturn finger: The second (middle) finger. A long Saturn finger signifies a potential for depression.

Saturn mount: The mount located just under the Saturn finger. If this mount is noticeably raised, it can mean the person suffers from chronic depression.

secondary line: Any line that appears alongside or near the major lines of the hand.

simian line: This line occurs at the merging point of two major lines, head and heart, and points to deep emotions or a physical affliction that leads to greater introspection.

spatulate: A rectangular shape that takes on the characterization of a spatula; can pertain to either finger or hand shape.

square shape: Hands and/or fingers that appear square in shape.

square mark: If this special marking appears on the palm, it offers the individual protection in the area associated with the nearest major line.

star: This unique marking can appear on any line or mount and can be a predictor or surprise, either happy or sad, depending on indications from other nearby lines.

travel line: Located near the bottom of the percussion of the hand, these lines indicate the type and length of travel or journeys in life.

triangle: A very lucky sign if it appears on the palm; indicates success beyond one's wildest dreams, along with the wisdom to handle it effectively.

Upper Mars mount: This mount, found between the Jupiter mount and the thumb, indicates whether a person is courageous (positive) or aggressive (negative).

Venus mount: A very popular mount in palmistry; located beneath the thumb, it indicates a person's sexual stamina and capacity for romance.

Via lascivia: This line, which can appear at the base of the percussion (near travel lines), is sometimes called the allergy line, since it can mean sensitivity to chemicals or airborne particles.

water hand: This hand type features a slender hand with long, pointed fingers. People with water hands are sensitive and sometimes secretive.

whorls: These secondary patterns, which can appear on both fingertips and palms, signify a closed mind or a person who is not open to new thoughts or ideas.

zones: Specific divisions of the hand; often broken down into quadrants.

Appendix B

Additional Resources

Books

Altman, Nathaniel. *The Palmistry Workbook*. (New York: Sterling Publishing Company, Inc., 1990)

_____. *The Little Giant Encyclopedia of Palmistry*. (New York: Sterling Publishing Company, Inc., 1999)

Anderson, Mary. *Understanding Palmistry*. (London: Thorsons, 1973)

Bashir, Mir. *The Art of Hand Analysis*. (London: Ashgrove Publishing, 2000)

Brenner, Elizabeth. *Hand in Hand*. (San Francisco: Celestial Arts, 1981)

_____. *The Hand Book*. (Sydney: Bay Books, 1980)

Broekman, Marcel. *The Complete Encyclopedia of Practical Palmistry*. (New York: Prentice Hall Press, 1972)

Bryden, Dean. *Palmistry for Pleasure*. (New York: George Sully and Co., 1926)

Campbell, Edward D. *The Encyclopedia of Palmistry*. (New York: Berkeley Publishing Group, 1996)

Casey, Carolyn W. *Making the Gods Work for You: The Astrological Language of the Psyche*. (New York: Three Rivers Press, 1999)

Cheiro. *The Language of the Hand*. (London: Corgi, reprint 1967)

_____. *Secrets of the Hand*. (Bombay: D.B. Taraporevala Sons & Co. Private Ltd., 1993)

Crosse, Joanna. *The Element Pocket Encyclopedia of Mind, Body, Spirit & Earth*. (Boston: Element Books, 1998)

Fitzherbert, Andrew. *Hand Psychology*. (Garden City, NY: Avery Publishing Group, Inc., 1989)

Douglas, Ray. *Palmistry and the Inner Self*. (London: Blandford, 1995)

Gerstein, Liz. *In the Palm of Your Hand*. (Carlsbad, CA: Hay House, 2002)

Gettings, Fred. *Palmistry Made Easy*. (London: Wilshire Book Company, 1966)

_____. *The Book of the Hand: An Illustrated History of Palmistry*. (London: Hamlyn, 1965)

Germain, Comte de Saint. *The Practice of Palmistry*. (New York: Newcastle Publications, 1973)

Gile, Robin and Lisa Lenard. *The Complete Idiot's Guide to Palmistry.* (Indianapolis, IN: Alpha Books, 1999)

Hazel, Peter. *Palmistry: Quick & Easy.* (St. Paul, MN: Llewellyn Publications, 2001)

Hipskind, Judith. *Palmistry: The Whole View.* (St. Paul, MN: Llewellyn Publications, 1988)

Hutchinson, Beryl. *Your Life in Your Hands.* (London: Sphere Books, Ltd., 1977)

Parker, Derek and Julia Parker. *The Future Now.* (New York: Prentice Hall Press, 1988)

Reid, Lori. *The Elements of Handreading.* (Boston: Element Books, LTD., 1994)

_____. *The Art of Hand Reading.* (New York: DK Publishing, Inc., 1999)

Robinson, Rita. *Discover Yourself Through Palmistry.* (Franklin Lakes, NJ: New Page Books, 2002)

St. Hill, Katherine. *Grammar of Palmistry.* (New Delhi: Sugar Publications, 1973)

Scheimann, Eugene. *Medical Palmistry: A Doctor's Guide to Better Health Through Hand Analysis.* (London: Aquarian Press, 1989)

Vaughan, Valerie. *Astro-Mythology: The Celestial Union of Astrology and Myth.* (London: One Reed Publications, 1999)

West, Peter. *Lifelines.* (New Delhi: Piper Press, 1973)

Whitaker, Hazel. *Palmistry: Your Highway to Life.* (Sydney: Lansdowne Publishing Pty. Ltd., 1998)

Wolff, Dr. Charlotte. *The Human Hand.* (New York: Meetheun & Co., 1942)

_____. Wolff, Dr. Charlotte. *Studies in Hand Reading.* (New York: Alfred A. Knopf, 1938)

Web Sites

International Institute of Hand Analysis
✏ www.handanalysis.net

This is the Web site of the International Institute of Hand Analysis, founded by Richard Unger. Here you'll find articles, book reviews, and other resources. You can also purchase newsletters, journals, and tapes published by the Institute.

Psychodiagnostic Chirology
✏ www.pdc.co.il/ind1.htm

This fascinating site supports the use of hand reading in psychological diagnosis.

Hand Analysis FAQ
✏ www.lynnseal.freeuk.com/faq.htm

Learn more about the myths, facts, and methods of palmistry.

Handscape.com
✏ www.handscape.com

This Web site is offered by author and palm reading expert Rita Robinson; it is chock full of terrific detail about the nuts and bolts of palm reading.

HumanHand.com
✏ www.humanhand.com

This Web site offers a wealth of information about palmistry.

The History of Handreading
✏ http://users.breathemail.net/chiro/chiro/

A very user-friendly site that explores virtually everything about palmistry and the ancient art of palm reading.

Palmistry Centre
✏ www.palmistry.com

The Web home of Quebec's famous Palmistry Centre, where you'll find tons of information on palmistry, articles, a detailed FAQ, information on classes offered at the center, and the opportunity to purchase related products.

Way Out There and Back
✏ www.wotab.co.uk

A great site where you can get a personalized palm chart online.

Index

The EVERYTHING Series!

BUSINESS & PERSONAL FINANCE

Everything® Accounting Book
Everything® Budgeting Book, 2nd Ed.
Everything® Business Planning Book
Everything® Coaching and Mentoring Book, 2nd Ed.
Everything® Fundraising Book
Everything® Get Out of Debt Book
Everything® Grant Writing Book, 2nd Ed.
Everything® Guide to Buying Foreclosures
Everything® Guide to Fundraising, $15.95
Everything® Guide to Mortgages
Everything® Guide to Personal Finance for Single Mothers
Everything® Home-Based Business Book, 2nd Ed.
Everything® Homebuying Book, 3rd Ed., $15.95
Everything® Homeselling Book, 2nd Ed.
Everything® Human Resource Management Book
Everything® Improve Your Credit Book
Everything® Investing Book, 2nd Ed.
Everything® Landlording Book
Everything® Leadership Book, 2nd Ed.
Everything® Managing People Book, 2nd Ed.
Everything® Negotiating Book
Everything® Online Auctions Book
Everything® Online Business Book
Everything® Personal Finance Book
Everything® Personal Finance in Your 20s & 30s Book, 2nd Ed.
Everything® Personal Finance in Your 40s & 50s Book, $15.95
Everything® Project Management Book, 2nd Ed.
Everything® Real Estate Investing Book
Everything® Retirement Planning Book
Everything® Robert's Rules Book, $7.95
Everything® Selling Book
Everything® Start Your Own Business Book, 2nd Ed.
Everything® Wills & Estate Planning Book

COOKING

Everything® Barbecue Cookbook
Everything® Bartender's Book, 2nd Ed., $9.95
Everything® Calorie Counting Cookbook
Everything® Cheese Book
Everything® Chinese Cookbook
Everything® Classic Recipes Book
Everything® Cocktail Parties & Drinks Book
Everything® College Cookbook
Everything® Cooking for Baby and Toddler Book
Everything® Diabetes Cookbook
Everything® Easy Gourmet Cookbook
Everything® Fondue Cookbook
Everything® Food Allergy Cookbook, $15.95
Everything® Fondue Party Book
Everything® Gluten-Free Cookbook
Everything® Glycemic Index Cookbook
Everything® Grilling Cookbook
Everything® Healthy Cooking for Parties Book, $15.95
Everything® Holiday Cookbook
Everything® Indian Cookbook
Everything® Lactose-Free Cookbook
Everything® Low-Cholesterol Cookbook

Everything® Low-Fat High-Flavor Cookbook, 2nd Ed., $15.95
Everything® Low-Salt Cookbook
Everything® Meals for a Month Cookbook
Everything® Meals on a Budget Cookbook
Everything® Mediterranean Cookbook
Everything® Mexican Cookbook
Everything® No Trans Fat Cookbook
Everything® One-Pot Cookbook, 2nd Ed., $15.95
Everything® Organic Cooking for Baby & Toddler Book, $15.95
Everything® Pizza Cookbook
Everything® Quick Meals Cookbook, 2nd Ed., $15.95
Everything® Slow Cooker Cookbook
Everything® Slow Cooking for a Crowd Cookbook
Everything® Soup Cookbook
Everything® Stir-Fry Cookbook
Everything® Sugar-Free Cookbook
Everything® Tapas and Small Plates Cookbook
Everything® Tex-Mex Cookbook
Everything® Thai Cookbook
Everything® Vegetarian Cookbook
Everything® Whole-Grain, High-Fiber Cookbook
Everything® Wild Game Cookbook
Everything® Wine Book, 2nd Ed.

GAMES

Everything® 15-Minute Sudoku Book, $9.95
Everything® 30-Minute Sudoku Book, $9.95
Everything® Bible Crosswords Book, $9.95
Everything® Blackjack Strategy Book
Everything® Brain Strain Book, $9.95
Everything® Bridge Book
Everything® Card Games Book
Everything® Card Tricks Book, $9.95
Everything® Casino Gambling Book, 2nd Ed.
Everything® Chess Basics Book
Everything® Christmas Crosswords Book, $9.95
Everything® Craps Strategy Book
Everything® Crossword and Puzzle Book
Everything® Crosswords and Puzzles for Quote Lovers Book, $9.95
Everything® Crossword Challenge Book
Everything® Crosswords for the Beach Book, $9.95
Everything® Cryptic Crosswords Book, $9.95
Everything® Cryptograms Book, $9.95
Everything® Easy Crosswords Book
Everything® Easy Kakuro Book, $9.95
Everything® Easy Large-Print Crosswords Book
Everything® Games Book, 2nd Ed.
Everything® Giant Book of Crosswords
Everything® Giant Sudoku Book, $9.95
Everything® Giant Word Search Book
Everything® Kakuro Challenge Book, $9.95
Everything® Large-Print Crossword Challenge Book
Everything® Large-Print Crosswords Book
Everything® Large-Print Travel Crosswords Book
Everything® Lateral Thinking Puzzles Book, $9.95
Everything® Literary Crosswords Book, $9.95
Everything® Mazes Book
Everything® Memory Booster Puzzles Book, $9.95

Everything® Movie Crosswords Book, $9.95
Everything® Music Crosswords Book, $9.95
Everything® Online Poker Book
Everything® Pencil Puzzles Book, $9.95
Everything® Poker Strategy Book
Everything® Pool & Billiards Book
Everything® Puzzles for Commuters Book, $9.95
Everything® Puzzles for Dog Lovers Book, $9.95
Everything® Sports Crosswords Book, $9.95
Everything® Test Your IQ Book, $9.95
Everything® Texas Hold 'Em Book, $9.95
Everything® Travel Crosswords Book, $9.95
Everything® Travel Mazes Book, $9.95
Everything® Travel Word Search Book, $9.95
Everything® TV Crosswords Book, $9.95
Everything® Word Games Challenge Book
Everything® Word Scramble Book
Everything® Word Search Book

HEALTH

Everything® Alzheimer's Book
Everything® Diabetes Book
Everything® First Aid Book, $9.95
Everything® Green Living Book
Everything® Health Guide to Addiction and Recovery
Everything® Health Guide to Adult Bipolar Disorder
Everything® Health Guide to Arthritis
Everything® Health Guide to Controlling Anxiety
Everything® Health Guide to Depression
Everything® Health Guide to Diabetes, 2nd Ed.
Everything® Health Guide to Fibromyalgia
Everything® Health Guide to Menopause, 2nd Ed.
Everything® Health Guide to Migraines
Everything® Health Guide to Multiple Sclerosis
Everything® Health Guide to OCD
Everything® Health Guide to PMS
Everything® Health Guide to Postpartum Care
Everything® Health Guide to Thyroid Disease
Everything® Hypnosis Book
Everything® Low Cholesterol Book
Everything® Menopause Book
Everything® Nutrition Book
Everything® Reflexology Book
Everything® Stress Management Book
Everything® Superfoods Book, $15.95

HISTORY

Everything® American Government Book
Everything® American History Book, 2nd Ed.
Everything® American Revolution Book, $15.95
Everything® Civil War Book
Everything® Freemasons Book
Everything® Irish History & Heritage Book
Everything® World War II Book, 2nd Ed.

HOBBIES

Everything® Candlemaking Book
Everything® Cartooning Book
Everything® Coin Collecting Book
Everything® Digital Photography Book, 2nd Ed.

Everything® Drawing Book
Everything® Family Tree Book, 2nd Ed.
Everything® Guide to Online Genealogy, $15.95
Everything® Knitting Book
Everything® Knots Book
Everything® Photography Book
Everything® Quilting Book
Everything® Sewing Book
Everything® Soapmaking Book, 2nd Ed.
Everything® Woodworking Book

HOME IMPROVEMENT

Everything® Feng Shui Book
Everything® Feng Shui Decluttering Book, $9.95
Everything® Fix-It Book
Everything® Green Living Book
Everything® Home Decorating Book
Everything® Home Storage Solutions Book
Everything® Homebuilding Book
Everything® Organize Your Home Book, 2nd Ed.

KIDS' BOOKS

All titles are $7.95
Everything® Fairy Tales Book, $14.95
Everything® Kids' Animal Puzzle & Activity Book
Everything® Kids' Astronomy Book
Everything® Kids' Baseball Book, 5th Ed.
Everything® Kids' Bible Trivia Book
Everything® Kids' Bugs Book
Everything® Kids' Cars and Trucks Puzzle and Activity Book
Everything® Kids' Christmas Puzzle & Activity Book
Everything® Kids' Connect the Dots
       Puzzle and Activity Book
Everything® Kids' Cookbook, 2nd Ed.
Everything® Kids' Crazy Puzzles Book
Everything® Kids' Dinosaurs Book
Everything® Kids' Dragons Puzzle and Activity Book
Everything® Kids' Environment Book $7.95
Everything® Kids' Fairies Puzzle and Activity Book
Everything® Kids' First Spanish Puzzle and Activity Book
Everything® Kids' Football Book
Everything® Kids' Geography Book
Everything® Kids' Gross Cookbook
Everything® Kids' Gross Hidden Pictures Book
Everything® Kids' Gross Jokes Book
Everything® Kids' Gross Mazes Book
Everything® Kids' Gross Puzzle & Activity Book
Everything® Kids' Halloween Puzzle & Activity Book
Everything® Kids' Hanukkah Puzzle and Activity Book
Everything® Kids' Hidden Pictures Book
Everything® Kids' Horses Book
Everything® Kids' Joke Book
Everything® Kids' Knock Knock Book
Everything® Kids' Learning French Book
Everything® Kids' Learning Spanish Book
Everything® Kids' Magical Science Experiments Book
Everything® Kids' Math Puzzles Book
Everything® Kids' Mazes Book
Everything® Kids' Money Book, 2nd Ed.
**Everything® Kids' Mummies, Pharaoh's, and Pyramids
       Puzzle and Activity Book**
Everything® Kids' Nature Book
Everything® Kids' Pirates Puzzle and Activity Book
Everything® Kids' Presidents Book
Everything® Kids' Princess Puzzle and Activity Book
Everything® Kids' Puzzle Book

Everything® Kids' Racecars Puzzle and Activity Book
Everything® Kids' Riddles & Brain Teasers Book
Everything® Kids' Science Experiments Book
Everything® Kids' Sharks Book
Everything® Kids' Soccer Book
Everything® Kids' Spelling Book
Everything® Kids' Spies Puzzle and Activity Book
Everything® Kids' States Book
Everything® Kids' Travel Activity Book
Everything® Kids' Word Search Puzzle and Activity Book

LANGUAGE

Everything® Conversational Japanese Book with CD, $19.95
Everything® French Grammar Book
Everything® French Phrase Book, $9.95
Everything® French Verb Book, $9.95
Everything® German Phrase Book, $9.95
Everything® German Practice Book with CD, $19.95
Everything® Inglés Book
Everything® Intermediate Spanish Book with CD, $19.95
Everything® Italian Phrase Book, $9.95
Everything® Italian Practice Book with CD, $19.95
Everything® Learning Brazilian Portuguese Book with CD, $19.95
Everything® Learning French Book with CD, 2nd Ed., $19.95
Everything® Learning German Book
Everything® Learning Italian Book
Everything® Learning Latin Book
Everything® Learning Russian Book with CD, $19.95
Everything® Learning Spanish Book
Everything® Learning Spanish Book with CD, 2nd Ed., $19.95
Everything® Russian Practice Book with CD, $19.95
Everything® Sign Language Book, $15.95
Everything® Spanish Grammar Book
Everything® Spanish Phrase Book, $9.95
Everything® Spanish Practice Book with CD, $19.95
Everything® Spanish Verb Book, $9.95
Everything® Speaking Mandarin Chinese Book with CD, $19.95

MUSIC

Everything® Bass Guitar Book with CD, $19.95
Everything® Drums Book with CD, $19.95
Everything® Guitar Book with CD, 2nd Ed., $19.95
Everything® Guitar Chords Book with CD, $19.95
Everything® Guitar Scales Book with CD, $19.95
Everything® Harmonica Book with CD, $15.95
Everything® Home Recording Book
Everything® Music Theory Book with CD, $19.95
Everything® Reading Music Book with CD, $19.95
Everything® Rock & Blues Guitar Book with CD, $19.95
Everything® Rock & Blues Piano Book with CD, $19.95
Everything® Rock Drums Book with CD, $19.95
Everything® Singing Book with CD, $19.95
Everything® Songwriting Book

NEW AGE

Everything® Astrology Book, 2nd Ed.
Everything® Birthday Personology Book
Everything® Celtic Wisdom Book, $15.95
Everything® Dreams Book, 2nd Ed.
Everything® Law of Attraction Book, $15.95
Everything® Love Signs Book, $9.95
Everything® Love Spells Book, $9.95
Everything® Palmistry Book
Everything® Psychic Book
Everything® Reiki Book

Everything® Sex Signs Book, $9.95
Everything® Spells & Charms Book, 2nd Ed.
Everything® Tarot Book, 2nd Ed.
Everything® Toltec Wisdom Book
Everything® Wicca & Witchcraft Book, 2nd Ed.

PARENTING

Everything® Baby Names Book, 2nd Ed.
Everything® Baby Shower Book, 2nd Ed.
Everything® Baby Sign Language Book with DVD
Everything® Baby's First Year Book
Everything® Birthing Book
Everything® Breastfeeding Book
Everything® Father-to-Be Book
Everything® Father's First Year Book
Everything® Get Ready for Baby Book, 2nd Ed.
Everything® Get Your Baby to Sleep Book, $9.95
Everything® Getting Pregnant Book
Everything® Guide to Pregnancy Over 35
Everything® Guide to Raising a One-Year-Old
Everything® Guide to Raising a Two-Year-Old
Everything® Guide to Raising Adolescent Boys
Everything® Guide to Raising Adolescent Girls
Everything® Mother's First Year Book
Everything® Parent's Guide to Childhood Illnesses
Everything® Parent's Guide to Children and Divorce
Everything® Parent's Guide to Children with ADD/ADHD
Everything® Parent's Guide to Children with Asperger's
       Syndrome
Everything® Parent's Guide to Children with Anxiety
Everything® Parent's Guide to Children with Asthma
Everything® Parent's Guide to Children with Autism
Everything® Parent's Guide to Children with Bipolar Disorder
Everything® Parent's Guide to Children with Depression
Everything® Parent's Guide to Children with Dyslexia
Everything® Parent's Guide to Children with Juvenile Diabetes
Everything® Parent's Guide to Children with OCD
Everything® Parent's Guide to Positive Discipline
Everything® Parent's Guide to Raising Boys
Everything® Parent's Guide to Raising Girls
Everything® Parent's Guide to Raising Siblings
**Everything® Parent's Guide to Raising Your
       Adopted Child**
Everything® Parent's Guide to Sensory Integration Disorder
Everything® Parent's Guide to Tantrums
Everything® Parent's Guide to the Strong-Willed Child
Everything® Parenting a Teenager Book
Everything® Potty Training Book, $9.95
Everything® Pregnancy Book, 3rd Ed.
Everything® Pregnancy Fitness Book
Everything® Pregnancy Nutrition Book
Everything® Pregnancy Organizer, 2nd Ed., $16.95
Everything® Toddler Activities Book
Everything® Toddler Book
Everything® Tween Book
Everything® Twins, Triplets, and More Book

PETS

Everything® Aquarium Book
Everything® Boxer Book
Everything® Cat Book, 2nd Ed.
Everything® Chihuahua Book
Everything® Cooking for Dogs Book
Everything® Dachshund Book
Everything® Dog Book, 2nd Ed.
Everything® Dog Grooming Book